D1645938

Economics, Enlightenment, and Canadian Nationalism

ROBERT W. WRIGHT

McGill-Queen's University Press
Montreal & Kingston • London • Buffalo

© McGill-Queen's University Press 1993
ISBN 0-7735-0979-8 (cloth)
ISBN 0-7735-0980-1 (paper)

Legal deposit third quarter 1993
Bibliothèque nationale du Québec

Printed in Canada on acid-free paper

This book has been published with the help of a grant
from the Social Science Federation of Canada, using
funds provided by the Social Sciences and Humanities
Research Council of Canada. Publication has also been
made possible, in part, by a grant provided by The
University of Calgary's General Endowment Fund and
by support from the Canada Council through its block
grant program.

Canadian Cataloguing in Publication Data

Wright, Robert W.
Economics, enlightenment, and Canadian nationalism
Includes bibliographical references and index.
ISBN 0-7735-0980-1 (bound)
ISBN 0-7735-0979-8 (pbk.)
1. Economics – Philosophy. 2. Progress.
3. Nationalism – Canada. I. Title.
HB72.W75 1993   330'.01   C93-090130-4

Excerpts of Margaret Atwood's poetry from *The
Animals in That Country, Power Politics, Two-Headed
Poems*, and *Interlunar* appear by permission of Oxford
University Press Canada.

Typeset in Palatino 10/12 by
Caractéra production graphique inc., Quebec City.

Contents

Preface / vii

1 Economic Man 3

2 A Flaw and a Remedy 23

3 Universal Knowledge 43

4 Local Knowledge 58

5 The Method 85

6 The Policies 99

7 A Summary 120

References 127

Index 133

Preface

What we observe is not nature itself but
nature exposed to our method of questioning.

The term "world-view" refers to the constellation of myths, symbols, beliefs, and organizing principles that give meaning to existence. A single world-view, sometimes called the *idea of progress*, has dominated Western society for three centuries. It has led to unprecedented technological change, material abundance, and apparent freedom. Simultaneously, a supportive institutional system has evolved to facilitate the exercise of its imperatives.

One of the most important elements of this system is the set of academic disciplines that provide the theories and the apologies for the *idea of progress*. Many of these disciplines trace their roots to the intellectual revolutions initiated by Descartes and Newton. Descartes proposed that nature can be understood by using reason if one relies on mathematics as an organizing and interpretive tool; Newton showed that nature is a mechanical system in which harmony prevails among particles and forces obeying understandable laws. Their shared belief that nature could and should be controlled to serve humanity's physical needs precipitated an epoch of discoveries in the physical sciences and the application of these discoveries to the realm of technology. Inevitably, scholars began to adapt the ideas and methods that seemed so successful in the physical sciences to the analysis of human behaviour. This was undoubtedly one of the most significant intellectual leaps in modern times. Not only did it establish the fields of inquiry now referred to as the social sciences but it led to methodological consistency across a broad spectrum of intellectual disciplines, so that they became mutually reinforcing components in the superstructure supporting the *idea of progress*.

The orthodox discipline of economics is one of the most important components in this superstructure. Its subject matter deals with the very essence of the *idea of progress*: optimizing behaviour, technological advance, control of nature, material abundance, and so on. Furthermore, it is a champion of the Descartes-Newton orientation, employing and advocating complex mathematical tools and constructing theories of action based on the axiom that harmony (equilibrium) is the goal of purposeful activity. Thus it can be said that orthodox economics is both a product and a proponent of the *idea of progress*.

Through time, the *idea of progress* has been repeatedly challenged by humanists, egalitarians, determinists, and environmentalists. Humanists are particularly critical of the failure to include moral values in the objective set of scientific inquiry, and they also argue that by restricting the domain of analysis to quantifiable variables, a destructive fragmentation emerges within both the physical and metaphysical worlds. These themes have been explored by many of the masters of literature from Swift to Tolstoy and Ibsen.

The *idea of progress* has also been challenged by egalitarians, who argue that it is a creed for the rich. Within the wealthiest nations the benefits of progress are shared unequally, and if one examines the issue in an international context, the distributional imbalance is even more pronounced. Many of those concerned about these inequities claim that it is the capitalist-imperialist orientation of the idea that is the villain. Marx is the principal proponent of this view.

Determinists argue that there is a fundamental flaw contained in the *idea of progress* paradigm. Specifically, it makes assumptions about the human condition that, in reality, are not innate but rather describe the consequences of living in a world dominated by the *idea of progress* itself. This flaw creates a situation in which pursuit of the idea reinforces the validity of its own assumptions but does not necessarily lead to an improvement in the human condition. Marx, Hegel, and an array of behaviourist psychologists have argued in this vein.

Environmentalists argue that orthodoxy ignores the inevitability of the entropy law as well as the adverse externalities associated with the addiction to energy-intensive lifestyles which accompany the *idea of progress*. They suggest that as a consequence, orthodoxy is an exercise concerned with short-run expediency rather than longer-run reality. This perspective is shared by contemporary scholars such as Lovins and Georgescu-Roegen.

Many of the criticisms articulated by humanists, egalitarians, determinists, and environmentalists have been directed specifically toward orthodox economics, in its role as a component in the superstructure

of the *idea of progress*. While the work of these reformers and icono-
clasts is characterized by prodigious energy and considerable insight,
their impact on the English-speaking world has not been great.
Orthodox economics remains intact and flourishes.

I have written this book because of the conviction that many of
these criticisms are warranted and in spite of past failures, the advocacy of fundamental reform must persist. Indeed, I shall argue that
orthodox economics is contributing to a debasement, rather than an
enhancement, of the human condition and that reform is a necessary
condition if true progress is to occur. Furthermore, if one searches
for the elements of effective transformation within a Canadian context, it becomes clear that any alternative to the orthodox formulation
must also be nationalistic. That is, if Canada is to create a social
arrangement that transcends the *idea of progress*, it must first distance
itself from the United States.

The complexities and possibilities of a transcendent Canadian
nationalism will be discussed in due course. However, at the outset
it is expedient to make a judgment about the continental environment
that the nation is likely to encounter in the foreseeable future. One
school of thought, represented by scholars such as Bell, Roszak, and
Lasch, warns that the present age is being driven by a disequili-
brating dynamic emanating from within the cultural realms of the
industrial nations which, when coupled with the forces generated by
international instabilities, may topple many traditional institutions in
the United States. If this upheaval is likely to occur, Canadian nationalism should perhaps be moulded with reference to an impending
American implosion. Alternatively, historians such as Polanyi and
Eksteins have noted that the *idea of progress* has always shown great
resilience in withstanding challenges to its fundamental modernist
orientation, and given this, homoeostatic processes can be expected
to continue to dominate social changes in America. I am inclined to
side with these latter scholars and therefore to conclude that Canadian nationalism will need to be actualized within an external environment characterized by dynamic stability rather than chaos.
However, this view does not necessarily simplify the task, for transcendence will still need to overcome formidable obstacles such as
conservatism, corporatism, and continentalism.

This book contains six chapters and a summary. The first chapter
inquires into the nature of orthodox economics in order to understand its anatomy and to appreciate both its capabilities and its
limitations. It is observed that the domain and the focus of the
discipline are shaped by a set of generic axioms which can be traced

back to the attempts by Smith and Ricardo to construct a scientific framework that was consistent with the world-views of Newton and Descartes. Paramount among these was the self-interest axiom, which eventually crystallized into *economic man*. As the discipline evolved to the present, this axiom and the scientific orientation became entrenched and its theoretical structures became pure rather than gestalt.

Chapter two points out that this orthodox perspective ignores deterministic (phenomenal) forces in the economic system and that there is evidence these forces are becoming increasingly influential as Western technology becomes more sophisticated. If this is the case, *economic man* is an output, as well as an initiator, of economic processes. As output, he should be evaluated, and if this is done, he is seen to be inferior. One way of resolving this deficiency is to modify the discipline by articulating a set of normatively satisfying statements about the human condition and then seek to design economic processes that will facilitate their realization. It is recognized that this type of disciplinary transformation is not an easy task because orthodoxy is supported by both its own adherents and other influential nodes in the superstructure of the *idea of progress*. However, there are reform mechanisms available, and one proposed by Foucault seems particularly promising. He urges an "insurrection of subjugated knowledges" involving a coalition of universal and local knowledges to confront orthodoxy.

Chapter three discusses universal knowledge, which is defined as the composite of ideas that give meaning to man's existence. Many intellectuals have investigated this concept throughout history, and there seems to be some consensus that the Bible provides the basic statement of Western universal knowledge. Frye argues that the dominant theme of the Bible is the myth of deliverance, and given this and the task of this inquiry, it seems reasonable to focus on those intellectuals who have postulated that it is from the *idea of progress* that contemporary man needs to be delivered. Many share this perspective, but there are three who seem to be particularly insightful: William Blake, Søren Kierkegaard, and Paul Tillich. Although separated in time, space, and the genre of expression, these three express a common belief about the conditions necessary for a meaningful existence and hence provide a plausible definition of universal knowledge.

Chapter four examines local knowledge, or the set of principles that should guide the national conscience. It is suggested that Margaret Atwood, Harold Innis, and Alex Colville have identified the main features of both our existence and our potential. In spite of the diversity of their intellectual orientation, they share the view that we are burdened with bias and domination: men over women, civilization over nature, space over time, centre over margin. Authenticity requires that we seek to eliminate the biases and establish tense dialectic relationships between these opposites. It is also concluded that if an economics discipline is to aid in this transition, it must be based on the kind of historically robust gestalt framework advocated by Innis.

Given our definitions of universal and local knowledge, it follows that the reformed discipline of economics should employ a dialectic methodology, because this approach reflects the realities of Canadian existence and also provides an appropriate framework for designing economic policies. While the dialectic method has a rich tradition, it has been overwhelmed by the scientific perspective of the *idea of progress* and has fallen into disuse, except amongst humanists. Chapter five describes the mechanics of dialectic analysis and illustrates how potent an intellectual tool it can be.

Chapter six discusses the policy recommendations that flow from the application of this new perspective. It is argued that the overall objective of eliminating domination in a variety of dimensions can best be accomplished if nationalism is assigned priority, because a geographic area can then be secured in which the other objectives can be nurtured by public policy. However, one must anticipate resistance to nationalism. It is suggested that much of this opposition is misguided and the result of perceiving reality through an alien paradigm. Furthermore, with specific reference to the economic consequences of nationalism, successful transition depends largely on the extent to which government policies can eliminate the inefficient distortions that currently exist in the economy. It is argued that existing policy levers can be recombined and redirected to serve the dual purpose of distancing us from the *idea of progress* and introducing sufficient competitive vitality to maintain our material standards. Once a nationalist environment is created, other biases in the Canadian system can be addressed and ameliorated by appropriate policy initiatives.

In this new disciplinary paradigm the principles of humanism, egalitarianism, and nationalism can coalesce. This situation arises because economic processes are designed with reference to their impact on human existence and not on material abundance. This is a major shift and requires that economists understand much more than we now do about the phenomenal and noumenal aspects of that existence. It may be that economics, like the new physics described by Capra, becomes the "study of the structure of consciousness."

I am grateful for support from the Social Science Federation of Canada for publication of this work, as well as for institutional support from the University of Calgary and the Hildebrant Library in Berlin. Elizabeth Hulse edited the manuscript with great sensitivity, and I sincerely appreciate her contribution. I also want to thank some colleagues and students who helped me in particularly significant ways: Frank, Stephen C., Judith, Moira, Robert, Cengiz, Bob, Petra, Scott, and especially Horst. Most importantly, I must thank Lorna and Donna for their guidance, inspiration, encouragement, and patience. This book is the result of a long journey that they made possible.

Finally, it should be noted that, except in the discussion of Atwood's work, the word "man" and its derivates refer generally to members of the human species and are gender neutral.

Economics, Enlightenment, and Canadian Nationalism

1 Economic Man

Gestalt theories are all alike; every pure theory
is pure in its own way.

The discipline of economics is concerned with the way that human beings produce, distribute, and consume the goods and services required to satisfy a particular subset of their needs and wants. While there have been various views about how the discipline's ideas and methods should be formulated and implemented, a single, mainstream orientation has emerged in the western world that is now characterized as orthodox economics.

Orthodox economics is evolutionary and has adjusted through time in response to changes in the production, distribution, and consumption systems that are the subject of its concern and to expansions in the state of knowledge. Since its inception, it has been dominated in turn by three different perspectives – classical, neoclassical, and Keynesian – which originated in the eighteenth, nineteenth, and twentieth centuries respectively. Each reached different conclusions about the relationship between economic variables and about the appropriate role of government in capitalistic societies.

There is a moderately interesting debate in the literature as to whether these transitions should be viewed as sharp paradigm shifts or whether orthodox economics has always retained a consistent intellectual core and merely resituated its perimeters. However, regardless of the way in which one wishes to conceptualize this evolution, it is obvious that both the ideas and the methods used by the discipline have changed over time. Primitive notions have been replaced by sophisticated theories, and increasingly complex techniques have been developed to test their veracity.

A more crucial debate concerns the difficulties of selecting an appropriate domain for analytic inquiry. All intellectuals recognize the need to be cognizant of the world they seek to understand, yet are in awe of its complexity. In attempting to explain even a subset of reality, say, those variables that affect economic processes, analysts have two alternative strategies. First, they may cast their net widely and seek to develop a single comprehensive theory which replicates the innumerable interactions that occur in the real economic world. However, this method soon becomes too cumbersome to be easily managed. Furthermore, it is very difficult to test the reasonableness of the conclusions that flow from theories fashioned in this way. For these reasons, such constructs, referred to as gestalt theories (Spiethoff 1953), are rarely formulated within the realm of orthodoxy.

More commonly, orthodox economists abstract from reality in order to isolate and analyse a limited number of variables. Normally, the selection of variables is based on the belief that their interrelationships are significant and not obvious and that the conclusions can be confirmed in some way. This latter condition requires that the included variables be quantifiable. A model thus constructed – in which aspects of reality are deliberately disregarded – is referred to as a pure theory.

One unfortunate implication of the tendency of orthodox economists to concentrate on pure theory is that it leads to ambiguity about the location of the boundaries of the discipline's domain. In the real world, economic processes are part of an immense network of social and natural systems, and there are no universal rules that divide this complex of interdependencies into a domain which is "economic" and one which is not. In spite of this ambiguity, it is useful to provide a crude representation of the discipline's boundaries, as in Figure 1, which suggests that reality is comprised of three categories or subsets: individuals, institutions, and the physical environment. Given this, it can be stated formally that the domain of orthodoxy is the intersection of these subsets, which includes those quantifiable variables that affect production, distribution, and consumption activities in a capitalistic system. Within this domain, pure theories are postulated to explain particular relationships, often augmented by intra-domain simplifying assumptions (Musgrave 1984), and are normally tested with reference to a logical or mathematical verification procedure. This format allows orthodox economics to qualify as a science.

A proponent of the *idea of progress* would undoubtedly argue that both orthodoxy and pure theory have made impressive contributions in showing how progress can be defined and achieved. However,

Figure 1
The Analytical Field

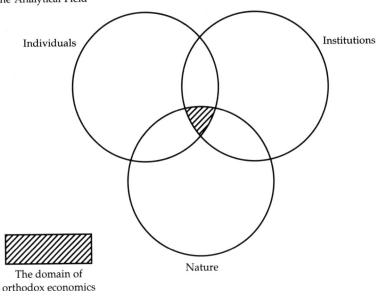

Individuals   Institutions

The domain of   Nature
orthodox economics

Figure 1 also highlights their limitations. First, the exclusion of non-domain variables limits the extent to which even verified theories can be applied to advantage. Indeed, most criticisms from alternative schools of thought – institutionalists, environmentalists, and humanists – are a consequence of the belief that the orthodox domain is too narrow. When economics is viewed in this way, many of the controversies within the discipline seem to relate simply to trade-offs between comprehensiveness and verifiability. Second, orthodoxy bifurcates entities. For example, a commodity is separated into its economic dimension, price, and an array of non-economic characteristics; similarly an individual is separated into an economic dimension, *economic man*, and an array of presumably unimportant, non-economic attributes. At a later stage it will be argued that this fragmentation, even for analytical purposes, is destructive to the human condition. At this point, it is sufficient to simply emphasize that one of the dominant silent leitmotifs of orthodoxy is that "purity fragments."

In any case, the domain of analysis is usually defined by a set of *generic axioms*, which are most often treated as data that do not require explanation. This practice has a long tradition, dating to the principles of discovery originally devised by Plato. In orthodox economics, these generic axioms normally include the following propositions:

- Truth is discovered through rational analysis.
- Individuals act in their own self-interest, as they perceive it.
- The natural state is one of harmony or equilibrium.
- Values can be defined in terms of market prices.
- Fairness is defined by the political system.
- Resources are scarce.

While these axioms may appear to be innocuous and even to fall into the category of self-evident truths, it is important to recognize that they have a pervasive effect on the character of the discipline. For example, it is the combination of the self-interest and scarcity axioms that leads to the focus on efficiency. Also, the practice of equating values with prices allows economists to ignore objects and sensations that are not exchangeable in markets. Furthermore, the fairness axiom allows them to avoid normative issues with impunity. In short, the generic axioms of orthodox economics are not neutral.

To summarize, it can be said that orthodox economics is an evolving discipline composed of an intertwining of ideas and methods, in which pure theory is developed and applied within a domain whose boundaries are defined by generic axioms.

Given this framework, the primary objective of this chapter is to discuss the significance of one of the axioms embedded in orthodoxy: the concept of *economic man*. The axiom will be shown to be immensely important because it facilitates a scientific–pure perspective rather than one that emphasizes humanistic-gestalt concerns, and this fact has a profound impact on the policy initiatives that flow from theoretical analysis. However, the axiom's origins can be traced to the eighteenth century, when it was innocently introduced simply to make the discipline consistent with the newly emerging *idea of progress*. Hence, it is useful to begin the discussion by examining this historical context.

THE IDEA OF PROGRESS

The eighteenth century was a time of intellectual ferment in western Europe, the character of which is captured by the various descriptors used by historians to identify the period: the Age of Reason, the Enlightenment, the Illumination, the Golden Age of Liberalism, and so on. The core idea was the belief that mankind is rational and that if left free, he can create an improved society. This view fostered a new climate of opinion, particularly amongst the intelligentsia: citizens developed confidence that their reasoning skills were sufficiently acute to interpret the world without reference to religious dogma or revelation; scientists discovered that nature functions like a machine and attempted to show that universal natural laws also exist in social arrangements; innovators devised technologies that shaped the environment to accommodate the imperatives of man's new perspective; in the political realm, there was a movement to expand the degree of electoral freedom and participation, in the interests of justice and enlightenment. The belief that these processes and concepts were feasible constituted the *idea of progress*; it shaped the western world.

Many intellectuals contributed to the creation of this new spirit. Two of the earliest and most influential forerunners were René Descartes and Isaac Newton. These scholars had a great impact on the classical economists Ricardo and Smith and hence on the axiomatic system that was eventually adopted by orthodox economics. For this reason it is instructive to discuss some of their ideas in detail.

Descartes, often called the father of Western philosophy, had a profound effect on all subsequent intellectual endeavour. However, the part of his work that was to be most relevant to economics can be summarized as a three-stage line of reasoning about how truth should be pursued. Specifically, he believed that

- the will of God is revealed through nature;
- nature is a system that obeys consistent laws;
- there is a preferred method for discovering these laws and hence for learning the truth about nature and the will of God.

It is useful to examine these three propositions separately, for each in its own right initiated an intellectual revolution and, in combination, a new world-view.

The idea that the will of God is revealed through nature challenged the medieval Christian dogma that presupposed a hierarchical universe in which individuals are ranked according to degrees of perfection and accordingly declared that truth is to be found in the revelations and pronouncements of the clerics and aristocrats at the apex of the social hierarchy. Descartes showed disdain for this belief and argued that the will of God is not revealed by fiat but rather through inquiry and discovery; furthermore, the best place to look for insights is in nature, for it is God's creation.

Descartes's second proposition, that nature obeys consistent laws, was also provocative because he warned that these laws are not always discernible to the senses. In fact, the senses are untrustworthy. For example, they interpret the world to be flat and stationary when it is round and spinning. For Descartes, we must learn about nature's laws "not by the prejudices of the senses but by the light of reason." This reliance on reason rather than the senses was to revolutionize the processes of intellectual inquiry.

However, his most creative and methodologically significant proposition related to the way in which man's reason is to be used to discover nature's laws. Descartes believed that identifiable components of physical reality (e.g., objects) should be *reduced to their mathematical properties* and logic used to analyse these properties in order to discover nature's essential relationships and forces. This idea, which is one of the landmarks of intellectual history, had two major effects on the process of inquiry. First, because the sum of the mathematical properties of an object does not equal the reality of the object (in subsequent terminology, the sum of the essences does not equal the existence), the world is divided into two realms: the web of concepts created in the mind about things (*res cogitans*) and things themselves (*res extensa*). Second, because the only essences of interest to a Cartesian are those that can be measured and manipulated mathematically, a hierarchy is created in the mind about the relative importance of different aspects of reality. Quantifiable characteristics take precedence over those related to such things as beauty and love.

Cartesianism had an indelible impact on the thought processes and behavioural patterns that gave momentum to the *idea of progress*. It is important to emphasize that the effect was both metaphysical and physical. To quote Mini,

the prime mover of Cartesianism was doubt and a skeptical attitude toward observation as a means of discovering the truth ... With this step, theorizing was anchored to the nature of the rationalistic thought process rather than the flux of evolving society.
... the logic of Cartesianism drives all thought towards fabricating a world in accordance with its own mathematical ideas of it. (Mini 1974, 284–5)

These two statements reveal a conceptual dilemma that Cartesians wrestle with to this day. That is, if theory is anchored in a particular reasoning process and abstracted from reality, yet seeks to shape this same reality, it must be normative and deterministic. Yet, most Cartesians like to think of themselves as positive, demonstrative scientists. How can this be?

The Cartesian system has also been subjected to other challenges. Theologians ask how one can be sure that the web of concepts created in the mind replicates the relationships which exist in reality and are answered, perhaps too cleverly, that it must be so because God is the creator of both the mind and reality and is not a deceiving God. Philosophers also ask why it is that only mathematical concepts matter and are answered, ingenuously, that if God has laws, they must be consistent and hence subject to measurable regularity. Consequently, they must also be amenable to description using the language of mathematics. In spite of such controversies, Cartesianism survives and flourishes as an integral component of the *idea of progress*.

Most economists, purblind to extra-disciplinary issues, have treated these fundamental dilemmas as peripheral nuances and have embraced the Cartesian system, although it is doubtful if many are aware of the full consequences of that embrace. Sceptical Cartesian economists might be particularly uneasy about some of the paradoxes that are included in their intellectual baggage. They will be aware that they have allowed mathematics to become the guardian of integrity, in spite of Lord Russell's observation that "mathematics can be defined as the subject in which we never know what we are talking about nor whether what we say is true." Furthermore, they may be uncomfortable in the realization that, because they are bringing the same habit of mind to the task of constructing and verifying any particular postulate, they are only proving that it is logical and not necessarily that it is true. Finally, they may be nervous about the various claims that economics is a positive, rather than a normative, science (Robbins 1935) when they often endow economic agents with the ability to make logical, rational decisions and then permit them to fashion reality according to this set of idealized principles. (A possible method of escaping from these dilemmas is to adopt a strict instrumentalist stance, although to do so implies that one must accept the role of a draftsman rather than an architect, and few are prepared to do so.)

The second major intellectual force of the era was Isaac Newton. He is renowned for his contributions to classical physics, his research methods, and his eclecticism (Keynes 1951, 310). He also developed calculus, which Einstein described as "perhaps the greatest advance in thought that a single individual was ever privileged to make," allowing man to explain and investigate the quantitative aspects of dynamic phenomena.

The Newtonian discovery that is probably most relevant to economics is his general conclusion that the laws of nature stabilize the objective world. This determination follows from a primary axiom identified as the first law of motion: every body continues in its state of rest, or in uniform motion in a straight line, unless it is compelled to change that state by forces impressed upon it. Given this, Newton sought to describe the gravitational forces that explain the non-linear movement of heavenly bodies. After doing so, he began an insightful process of *extension*, showing that earthly objects are subject to the same gravitational forces and hence that large tracts of experience are united by a few, relatively simple physical principles. Thus, what appears to be a chaotic state of nature is in actuality a harmonious set of relationships between entities obeying the same laws. Further, he believed that his conceptualization had universal applicability across an even wider range of environmental and social phenomena than he had discovered, stating, "I wish we could derive the rest of the phenomena of Nature by the same kind of reasoning from mechanical principles. For I am induced by many reasons to suspect that they may all depend on certain forces by which ... bodies ... are either mutually impelled toward one another ... or are repelled" (Newton 1968, Preface). This suggestion that the laws of nature might also apply to social relations provided the gateway through which the Newtonian world-view eventually entered the social sciences and the axiomatic structure of orthodox economics.

A second aspect of Newton's perspective that was to become a central focus of the *idea of progress* and of orthodox economics was his method. Newton wanted to both construct and verify theories with reference to observed reality (although he sometimes lapsed from his own standards). This concern brought him into an interesting juxtaposition with Descartes. They agreed on many things: the merits of Aristotelian circularity between induction and deduction in the discovery process, the existence of natural laws as the ultimate expression of God's will, and the primacy of mathematics as the appropriate mechanism for both revealing and explaining these laws. However, they differed fundamentally on the correct way of verifying theories. This difference has caused a split among the intellectuals who foster the *idea of progress*: Cartesians are identified as rationalists or apriorists (Machlup 1978, 141) and Newtonians as empiricists. The methodological split continues to exist in orthodox economics.

However, the similarities between Descartes and Newton are much more important than their differences. Together they forged a perspective which gave mankind confidence that if we use our reasoning ability, we will be able to understand natural laws and hence God's will. This conviction, reinforced with a sprinkling of the Protestant ethic (Weber 1985), inevitably led to the belief that we can also design our environment so as to create a more noble existence.

The confidence in our ability to improve reality through design, referred to by Hayek as "constructive rationalism," became the essential element of the *idea of progress*. It was conceived in the belief that if rationality can discover the truth, it should also be an effective mechanism for reconstructing the world. While humanists wept at the implications of this belief, it carried the day. Hayek summarized the issue by stating, "This 'rationalist' approach ... produced a renewed propensity to ascribe the origin of all institutions of culture to invention or design. Morals, religion and law, language and writing, money and the market, were thought of as having been deliberately constructed by somebody, or at least as owing whatever perfection they possessed to such design" (Hayek 1973, 10). If society had been created by design, it could be improved by a better design. The *idea of progress* was launched.

This new world-view permeated all intellectual disciplines. In the social sciences, John Locke (1924, 1967) was one of the first proselytizers. He is of particular interest because he treated acts of faith as axiomatic laws. (See Parry 1978, 12.) Furthermore, he melded the ideas of rationality, natural law, and harmony into a plausible theory about optimal political arrangements. Because he also included self-interest as a variable in his inquiries, he provided a model for the classical economists.

THE CLASSICAL ECONOMISTS

The term "classical economics" refers to the ideas of a group of British intellectuals who, between 1775 and *circa* 1850, applied the principles of Descartes and Newton and the lessons of Locke to the study of economic phenomena. Their most significant contribution was the construction of a theory which indicates that resources are used most efficiently and human welfare is maximized if production takes place in freely competitive markets.

One of the more interesting aspects of the movement is the manner in which the world-views of the two founders, Adam Smith and David Ricardo, were imprinted on later thought patterns. Smith had an empiricist orientation and introduced concepts such as self-interest into the discipline in a Locke-like attempt to situate economics in a Newtonian version of the *idea of progress*. His discourses are penetrating but not unambiguous, for there is occasional imprecision about the definitions of the domain, variables, and axioms under discussion. On the other hand, Ricardo was a Cartesian who, while accepting many of Smith's tenets, sought to construct more formal theories within a well-defined framework. Thus, orthodox economics was born as a hybrid combination of the Newton-Smith and Descartes-Ricardo paradigms. As the discipline evolved, these two strains can still be identified, with the former reflected most often in ideas and the latter in method.

If one examines the corpus of Smith's work, it becomes apparent that he, perhaps more than anyone else, sought to impose the spirit of the *idea of progress* on the study of economic phenomena. Approaching this task he was mindful of the fact that the organizing principle of any new discipline is generally an adaptation of a similar principle from some more mature art or science. In the application of this "discovery by analogy" strategy, Smith chose Newton as his mentor and natural law as his model. With respect to Newton, he stated,

Can we wonder then, that [Newton's system] should have gained the general and complete approbation of mankind, and that it should now be considered, not as an attempt to connect in the imagination the phenomena of the Heavens, but as the greatest discovery that ever was made by man, the discovery of an immense chain of the most important and sublime truths, all closely connected together, by one capital fact, of the reality of which we have daily experience. (Smith 1963, 189)

Further, he was convinced that the harmonious mechanistic attributes of the Newtonian system were particularly appropriate as an explicans of social processes. He stated, "Human society, when we contemplate it in a certain abstract and philosophical light, appears like a great, an immense machine, whose regular and harmonious movements produce a thousand agreeable effects" (Smith 1976, 316).

This idea permeates both of Smith's major works, *The Theory of Moral Sentiments* and *The Wealth of Nations*. (See Thompson 1965.) In the former, harmonious equilibrium is maintained between the individual and society by sympathy (i.e., compassion), which constrains human activities and directs actions into a pattern that is consistent with the laws of nature. In the latter book, it is maintained in the economic system by the invisible hand.

Every individual ... endeavors ... to employ his capital [so that] its produce may be of greatest value ... He generally ... neither intends to promote the public interest, nor knows how much he is promoting it ... he intends only his own security, ... only his own gain, and he is in this ... led by an invisible hand to promote an end which is no part of his intention ... By pursuing his own interest he frequently promotes that of the society more effectually than when he really intends to promote it. (Smith 1937, 423)

In short, self-interest imparts the motion in society while sympathy and the invisible hand direct that motion toward worthwhile ends.

It is wise to pause here because this idea of self-interest was eventually to be translated into *economic man* within the orthodox axiomatic structure, and it is important to ensure that Smith is interpreted fairly. At the outset, it should be noted that, while he was not the first person to draw attention to the significance of self-interest in economic processes, he was more insightful than his predecessors (Viner 1960). Also, it is important to situate Smith correctly in the nature-nurture controversy that haunts the social sciences. Generally, he seemed to believe that self-interest is a propensity which "comes with us from the womb" and which therefore is implanted within us as an artifice of Nature. Hollander (1977) has explored Smith's work in depth and shows that whereas he did not prove that self-interest is intrinsic in any rigourous scientific way, he provided numerous illustrations (of butchers, brewers, bakers, hunters, shepherds, freemen, slaves, feudal lords and serfs, Dutchmen, Englishmen, and Scots, etc.) to demonstrate its universality. While his statement that "the concrete social environment must also be taken into consideration in explaining the nature of the individual man" indicates that he was aware of the existence of deterministic elements, they were not given prominence. Finally, it should also be noted that Smith believed the eventual goal of self-interest is refinement: an expansion in the variety, the beauty, and the enlightenment associated with human life. It is not to be directed toward the mindless pursuit of individual wealth.

However, progress is said to require that this natural human propensity be allowed to operate without artificial restraint. This concept became the credo for the capitalistic system, which has provided the superstructure for the *idea of progress*. It is not our purpose to discuss how Smith's ideas became the foundation upon which the edifice of market capitalism was constructed; it is a complex issue because, in one of the great ironies of intellectual history, Smith had an effect that was no part of his original intention. However, there are two smaller, more specific points about what Smith actually said that should be addressed briefly. First, competition must exist if a social arrangement based on the invisible hand is to be progressive and stable over the long run. Without competition, the system is indeterminate and potentially unstable in the same way that the solar system would be unstable if one of the planets were to change its orbit and be directed by its own will. Second, there is debate as to whether the market system described by Smith should be viewed as a normative, or a positive, construct. Some argue that it was a plea to reform the British commercial system in order to make it consistent with a particular view of human nature and human potentiality (Rogin 1956). Others argue that it was a positive inquiry to reveal the long-run conditions of existence, based on the realities of history, psychology, and logic. This controversy remains unresolved.

Our discussion leads to the following conclusion about Smith. In his formulation, self-interest is the critical force that brings economic behaviour into the mainstream of both the *idea of progress* and the laws of nature. Harmony and progress are engendered externally by competition and internally by a motivational structure that includes elements of sympathy and the quest for refinement. These forces have the same stabilizing effect on the social system as gravitation has on the stellar system. While Smith recognized an element of environmental determinism in human affairs, it does not take on major significance. Man has free will to shape his own destiny; like Locke, Smith believed that he will do so rationally and creatively.

If Smith is assessed with reference to Figure 1, it seems that the domain of his analysis is quite extensive. He discussed the interactions between economic, political, and social institutions; his economic agents are endowed with an array of motivations, and while they are specialized, they are not fragmented; he included elements of the physical environment in his explanations. He was a person of global interests and his economic paradigm reflects this eclecticism.

However, in the post-Smith era, the domain of classical economics began to narrow. An early shrinkage occurred in response to the debates between David Ricardo and Thomas Malthus. Ricardo argued that economic propositions should normally be evaluated by examining the logic involved in their formulation, while Malthus wanted to evaluate propositions within the context of the history and institutional structure of the society in question. It was a manifestation of the rationalist-empiricist debate that was occurring simultaneously between Cartesians and Newtonians in the larger intellectual community. In economics, Ricardo carried the day and his method of analysis became the standard for subsequent generations.

The essence of the Ricardian method is simplification and abstraction. This process can be illustrated by examining the line of reasoning he used to arrive at his theory of value: that the exchange ratio of goods is determined by their labour content. Previously, Smith had discussed this issue but had been imprecise because of the difficulties of isolating the separate contributions of land, capital, and labour in making up the value of the commodity produced. Ricardo approached the problem by simply defining land and capital so that they have no bearing on value. That is, land is seen to be of variable quality but in fixed supply and subject to diminishing returns. As cultivation is pushed by population pressure to marginal land that receives no rent, again by definition it can be logically deduced that rent does not enter into agricultural prices. Also, capital is defined as embodied labour and hence is reduced to its labour equivalent. (Capital is entitled to a profit for the delay in returns necessitated by the length of the production period, but Ricardo did not allow this fact to interfere with his theory.) Consequently, a commodity's value can be expressed in terms of its labour content alone. In short, Ricardo introduced a style of analysis in which complex economic issues are reduced to their primary, quantifiable causal relationships.

Abstraction and deduction were also used to formulate his theory of comparative advantage. Here it is assumed that a situation exists involving two countries, two commodities, constant returns, perfect competition, and no institutional impediments or imbalances in political power, and allowing only for differences in technology, he shows that free trade benefits both nations. It was a landmark theory in economics which, for example, underpins the Canadian interest in free trade. It is also a testament to the fact that the impact of a theory need not be related to the truth of its assumptions.

Ricardo is revered for his ideas, but for our purposes it is his method that is most relevant. He introduced a habit of mind into economics in which theories are formulated on the basis of a few precisely stated axioms, and relationships are evaluated, not by empirical verification or with reference to realism, but rather by examining their internal logic. Deane summarizes his contribution as follows:

If one were to try to account for the importance of Ricardo in the development of economic thought ... one does not find the answer either in the 'topical' character of his message, or in the originality of his ideas or concepts, nor even in the superiority of his theoretical analysis. It lies rather in his capacity to construct out of familiar conceptual material a simple, consistent, and (within its limits) logically satisfying macroeconomic system ... He showed for the first time how a simple analytical model of the economy, operating with a very few, precisely defined, readily intelligible, strategic variables, could be employed to analyze complex economic processes and justify unambiguous policy prescriptions. (Deane 1978, 79)

It should be noted that even though Ricardo's theories are based on abstractions, he did not hesitate to apply his conclusions to real-world situations. This willingness to leap from metaphysical fantasy to physical reality is referred to as the "Ricardian vice."

However, perhaps the most important indirect impact of the Ricardian perspective arises from his practice of focusing on the acquisitive aspects of man's character. As a result, the discipline's human-condition axiom changed from Smith's self-interest–sympathy–refinement concept to the wealth-maximizing agent who was eventually to become crystallized as *economic man*. With Ricardo, economics took a step away from holism and began to think of a fragmented fictional human character as its subject matter.

This orientation was accepted by other classical writers. Jeremy Bentham (1948) postulated that man is a utility maximizer, seeking pleasurable experiences and avoiding painful ones, and that money is the best available instrument for measuring the intensity of desires and sensations. That is, money is a universal yardstick. (As an aside, it is interesting to note that Bentham, like Smith, had an effect that was no part of his original intention. He was a non-Cartesian reformer who contributed to an intensification of Cartesianism because his ideas of money and utility fit so nicely into that mould.) The hedonist element was reinforced by Nassua Senior (1951), who wrote that a comprehensive theory of economics could be deduced by reasoning from four basic postulates, one of which was that "man desires to obtain wealth with as little sacrifice as possible."

However, it was John Stuart Mill who finally formalized the fictional character nurtured by Ricardo, Senior, and Bentham into what is now recognized as *economic man*. He insisted that if political economy is to be taken as a serious science economists must be prepared to reason from assumed premises that may or may not be realistic. In the case of the axiom about the human condition, this process requires fragmentation.

Political economy does not treat of the whole of man's nature as modified by the social state, nor the whole conduct of man in society. It is concerned with him solely as a being who desires to possess wealth, and who is capable of judging of the comparative efficiency of means for obtaining that end. (See Machlup 1978, 104.)

Mill was careful to point out that the abstraction thus conceptualized was a fiction but was necessary because "this is the way in which science must necessarily proceed. When an effect depends on a concurrence of causes, those causes must be studied one at a time"

(Mill 1968, 139). The important attribute of the single cause of behaviour which Mill chose to isolate was that it is amenable to mathematical analysis. This decision had a pervasive effect on the nature of the discipline which subsequently evolved.

The practice that Mill advocated moved economics more and more into the realm of pure theory. Abstraction and the *ceteris paribus* safety net became common tools of analysis. The blind spot of the age was the failure to recognize that the theories are fictions and that it is perilous to apply the conclusions to the real world. Spiethoff's (1953) warning that "the value which the results [of pure theory] have for the explanation of economic reality depends critically on the way the problems are posed and upon the nature of the underlying axioms" went largely unheeded. This is particularly true of the *economic man* axiom, which proved to be so useful to the pure theorists of the era.

It is also interesting to note that the narrowing of the discipline of economics and the elevation of *economic man* to become a primary element in the analytical system paralleled the narrowing of the focus of the real world's *idea of progress* toward materialism at the expense of such characteristics as refinement and sympathy. Polanyi (1944) argues that the history of the nineteenth century was dominated by a clash between an emerging market economy and the resistance of those classes whose welfare was adversely effected by the transformation. In this clash, market interests prevailed, so that those motivated primarily by the pursuit of wealth became increasingly powerful. Although I do not wish to infer the direction of any causal relationships between the discipline of economics and the economic world, the increasing materialism of the industrial regime undoubtedly lent support to the use of the *economic man* construct because economists could claim to be not only scientific, but also positivist.

THE NEO-CLASSICAL EXTENSION

After 1850 three fundamental changes occurred in the classical model which led to a new school of economic thought, since referred to as neo-classicism. The first arose because there was a shift in the intent of economic analysis. Whereas the classical economists are uncompromising advocates of individualism, neo-classicists take the free market as a given and concern themselves with price formation within such a system. Second, the neo-classicists give more weight to demand considerations, and by presenting a balanced view of production and consumption they can, with legitimacy, claim to have a more comprehensive perspective. Third, they attach much greater relevance to the margin. This development has wide-reaching implications because the marginal idea is both amenable to sophisticated mathematics and applicable to a large number of concepts (e.g., costs, revenue, utility, productivity, etc.); hence, it provides a means of integrating many diverse variables into a single framework.

The neo-classical shift to detailed analysis of market behaviour and the emphasis on mathematics meant that *economic man* becomes an even more useful axiom. Furthermore, there were other forces operating that served to reinforce his central position, namely, the entwining of a mutually supporting set of complementary axioms to define the domain of the new mathematical perspective. Perhaps the most significant of these new axioms is the assumption of long-run equilibrium. Newtonian harmony is resurrected in microeconomics by Alfred Marshall, who showed that the quantity of a good demanded is set where the marginal utility of the good is in equilibrium with the marginal utility of the money required to purchase it. In macroeconomics, Leon Walras constructed an elegant mathematical model in which equilibrium is achieved simultaneously in all good and factor markets. This model was to become a major analytical tool in the discipline even though it is a pure and potentially misleading abstraction. As one critic has observed, "If one was to visualize the system at work, one would have to imagine a group of faceless and unrelated individuals gathering in a market place occasionally nodding their heads and vanishing into thin air ... [This] is hardly a meaningful abstraction of a complex industrial economy" (Katouzian 1980, 28). This interpretation of equilibrium strengthened the worthiness of *economic man*, not only because it helped to codify abstraction but because it created the illusion that the two are complementary. If one wishes to contribute to long-run harmony, one should be materialistic.

Another methodological nuance that indirectly strengthened the tendency to maintain *economic man* within the discipline's axiomatic structure was the drift toward positivism. This is a word that has many meanings, but there are two interpretations that are particularly important in economics: with respect to intent, one can distinguish between positive (what is) and normative (what ought to be); with respect to testing the plausibility of a theory, one can distinguish between positive methods (empirically verifiable or falsifiable) and analytic methods (aprioristic and logically verifiable).

Most neo-classical economists sought to be positive rather than normative (Robbins 1935) in the general belief that they have no particular right or aptitude to make moral judgements about the behaviour of others except, of course, if it involves efficiency! Given this and the fact that the discipline's subject matter had narrowed to a concentration on market behaviour, positive economists were very comfortable with the *economic man* axiom, because that is what they observed. Even when people are seen to behave in some other way, the economist can fall back on Neville Keynes's argument that the discipline should admit that its predictive capabilities are limited and that it should view itself as a science concerned with long-run tendencies. Thus, perturbations and anomalies can be ignored without admitting to the Ricardian vice.

The impact of the neo-classical positive versus analytic controversy is more difficult to assess. It was the contemporary economic manifestation of the Newton versus Descartes debate, which is embedded in the *idea of progress*. During the later neo-classical period and extending to the present day, the positivist perspective has been in the ascendency. Several factors have contributed to this trend, including the emergence of the logical-positivist school of philosophers, who established a higher degree of credibility for empirical work (Caldwell 1982); the growth of econometrics, which, though it often confuses causation and correlation, nevertheless enhances the reputation of empirical research programs; and the post-war dominance of the positivistic "Chicago school" in intellectual circles (Reder 1982). Nevertheless, Cartesian-style analytical methods continue to thrive. In fact, a recent analysis of the content of scholarly publications indicated that more than half were "mathematical models without data," a very definite Cartesian category (Leontief 1982).

While the positive versus analytic debate has undoubtedly influenced the direction of economic research, it has done nothing to weaken the *economic man* axiom. Both methods thrive on the quantifiable interpretation of human motivation and the optimizing behaviour implicit in the axiom. Furthermore, as the real world adopted an increasingly materialistic interpretation of the *idea of progress*, the heuristic fiction of the analytical school comes more and more to resemble the real economic agents of positivism.

For all these reasons, the idea of *economic man* flourished during the neo-classical period. While some were concerned that man was being too narrowly defined (Wicksteed 1933), this view was dismissed in the rush to develop precise, quantifiable laws within a pure theoretical framework. In 1880 Walter Bagehot reiterated Mill's principle, stating,

Political economy deals not with the entire real man as we know him in fact, but with a simpler imaginary man ... The abstract man of this science is engrossed with one desire only – the desire of possessing wealth ... because it is found convenient to isolate the effects of this force from all others. (Bagehot 1888, 74)

The mould was cast.

KEYNES

The most significant policy conclusion of neo-classical theory is that the role of government can be minimized and that the pace and direction of economic development can be left to market forces without violating the tenets of the *idea of progress*. The most serious challenger to this conclusion (aside from Marx) is John Maynard Keynes, certainly the most influential economist of this century. My intent is not to describe the Keynesian revolution as such but rather to use him to illustrate that the narrow, scientific orientation of the discipline had by this time become so entrenched it was able to repel or modify criticism without altering its basic form. Marcuse (1964) has said that the distinguished characteristic of capitalism is its infinite capacity to absorb social change without altering its basic exploitive structure. Similarly, orthodox economics has developed the capacity to absorb serious criticism while preserving its own scientific structure. It too has learned to deflect and co-opt.

Keynes is not only the most influential economist of the century but possibly the most often misrepresented. He felt that economics should be viewed as a prelude to the practice of moral acts, yet his work led to an increase in the degree to which economics is isolated from philosophy. He viewed the essence of the economic problem to be related to distributional struggles between the classes, yet his theories became guidelines for the preservation of the *status quo*. He was concerned about the quality of government, yet his name is associated with the quantitative dimensions of public finance. He debunked the notion of equilibrium, yet well-intentioned disciples modified his theories so that they could be conceptualized in equilibrium terms. These various paradoxes provide scope for many different lines of inquiry. However, as indicated, our discussion is confined to issues related to *economic man* and the appropriate domain of economic analysis.

Keynes was an empiricist. His views about economics are conditioned by his underlying belief that theory should be rooted in the facts of experience and that one of the most pervasive of these facts is the existence of uncertainty. He believed that uncertainty normally precludes the possibility of consistent, calculating, maximizing behaviour among economic agents, even when they are trying to increase their own wealth, income, or utility. Some scholars have suggested that his pragmatism can be traced to the disillusionment of his wartime experiences, as expressed in *The Economic Consequences of the Peace*, when he was dismayed to discover that tremendously important decisions related to the peace treaty of 1919 were based on hunches and obscure historical interpretations rather than on rational analysis, as the term is normally defined.

Given this, while Keynes did not doubt the ubiquity of materialistic egocentricity, he felt that its essence is not captured by the standard *economic man* axiom, in which uncertainty is either ignored or turned into a symmetrical distribution of risks around a mean, which is then treated as a certainty equivalent. (He had disdain for this latter practice, arguing that the "assumption of arithmetically equal probabilities based on a state of ignorance leads to absurdities.") Keynes's experiences made him aware that under conditions of uncertainty, decisions are usually based on psychic states and attitudes that can be best understood within a gestalt frameword. (See Cain 1984.) His attitude is illustrated in his explanation of investment behaviour. Under conditions of uncertainty, various forces converge into a "state of confidence" that typically becomes the basis for the investor's action. This state is continuously subjected to shocks, but even when there is stability, action is guided by convention rather than calculation. Because this method of responding to uncertainty is idiosyncratic and multidimensional, the simple characteristics ascribed to *economic man* are not of sufficient complexity to explain the nature of economic decisions. The issue then is not the absence of self-interest, but rather the inability to anticipate how it is reflected in behaviour in an uncertain world.

Keynes also had unorthodox views about the concept of equilibrium. In a world where buyers and sellers are uninformed about each other's activities, it is highly unlikely that all expectations will be realized and all markets will clear. Consequently, the economy is in a chronic state of *disequilibrium*. His view was that "we oscillate, avoiding the gravest extremes of fluctuations in employment and in prices in both directions, around an intermediate position appreciably below full employment" (Keynes 1935, 254). These oscillations are inherent in the economic system, and to the extent that stability is possible, it relates to the limitations of fluctuations and not, as the neo-classicals proposed, to the achievement of a long-term steady state.

However, Keynes's plea for a gestalt-disequilibrium orientation for economic analysis was unsuccessful. His followers sought to take what they believed to be his main idea – the fact that a free-market economy is unlikely to generate full employment – and to recast it so that it would be compatible with the orthodox framework. As Davidson has observed,

While Keynes was still attempting to refine this new way of viewing economic phenomena ... a number of other economists were trying to comprehend Keynes' ideas in terms of traditional theory. Hicks published a "potted version" of what he believed to be Keynes' central argument, using the famous IS-LM diagram of a general equilibrium system. This began a retrograde movement of modification, alteration, and distortion of the new paradigm to force it into the older neoclassical mold. (Davidson 1977, 276)

In the post-Keynesian era, the hard core of orthodoxy seems to have reverted to the neo-classical formulation, with opposition to discretionary monetary and fiscal policy, emphasis on prediction rather than explanation, and advocacy of a positivist research program. However, there has been considerable slippage from this formulation. That is, there are many who support intervention and normative analysis and who seek to persuade and to explain phenomena. As a consequence there is some blurring of the boundaries of orthodoxy with respect to both objectives and methods, and a rich literature in which these issues are discussed. (See Blaug 1980, Caldwell 1982, and Mirowski 1988.) Through all this development, a single principle remains inviolate: the mission of orthodoxy is to facilitate the continuing evolution of the *idea of progress* and the market system that is its creation and guardian. The *economic man* axiom remains as an effective servant in this endeavour.

2 A Flaw and a Remedy

Normative theorizing, while contrary to the spirit of the age,
is consistent with the spirit of the species.

In this chapter some of the criticisms of orthodoxy's *economic man* axiom will be examined, with attention focused on the concerns expressed by determinists. Their basic argument is that *economic man* is endowed with free will and that this is a simplified and misleading interpretation of the human condition.

The argument is a manifestation of the nature versus nurture debate which has intrigued scholars for centuries. This debate has numerous structural and definitional nuances but if we use Kant's (1905) terminology, the essence of the controversy can be put simply: man is a composite in which some elements are shaped by his environment and history (phenomena) and some by his voluntary actions (noumena). Man as phenomenon is determined, while man as noumenon has free will. Nobody disputes that these two elements coexist; rather, the dispute is about their relative importance and the implications of the interactions that occur between them.

The various versions of the paradigm of orthodox economics are almost all built on the premise that man is a noumenal creature who freely designs his environment to achieve materialistic objectives and that the only relevant phenomenal constraints are those related to physical laws and his own ignorance. This formulation ignores a whole subset of phenomenal forces that are generated by man's own economic creations and which influence his behaviour. For example, it could be that some of the characteristics ascribed to *economic man* are the result of forces generated by the *idea of progress* and are not totally immanent to mankind itself. If this is the case, and if these forces are significant, a serious flaw exists within the orthodox paradigm that destroys its integrity even though its internal logic stays intact. In order to assess the seriousness of this deficiency, it is useful to review some of the theories that have been developed about the nature of the phenomenal forces generated within Western industrial society. It is convenient to categorize these under three headings:

- global theories which indicate that there is something inherent in the *idea of progress* which makes intentional (i.e., those originating in human action) deterministic forces significant;
- technological theories which indicate that these forces are becoming increasingly significant over time because of the nature of technological change;
- erosion theories which indicate that these forces gain strength by eroding the institutions which are essential for the exercise of free will.

At the outset it should be emphasized that these categories intersect and that the list of theoreticians to be discussed is neither exhaustive nor exclusive. The purpose is not to present a definitive taxonomy of intentional deterministic theories; rather, it is to inquire as to whether deterministic forces are of sufficient importance to justify their inclusion in the paradigms of those intellectual disciplines that purport to contribute to an understanding of contemporary reality.

GLOBAL THEORIES

One of the earliest global theories was advanced by Thomas Hobbes, who, "widely and rightly regarded as the most formidable of English political theorists" (Macpherson 1962, 9), wrote in the seventeenth century about the nature of man and the qualities of an optimal political system. Although he predates the *idea of progress*, he deserves mention because many theories developed subsequently are just variations on his theme.

Hobbes wrote at a time when the spirit of individualism and a market mentality were emerging in England (Macfarlane 1979), and he sought to explain these occurrences. He began by examining a hypothetical situation in which laws and authority are removed from a civilized society in such a way that the previously acquired civil behaviour persists. The result is man in his natural state, although it is important to recognize that this is not a Swiftian yahoo but rather a creature with some degree of refinement operating in a primitive market system. In this state, man is said to possess three natural dispositions: competitiveness, diffidence, and the desire for recognition. These can all be accommodated by the pursuit of wealth, so man desires to live commodiously. However, in a world of scarcity to do so requires competitive action, and even those "that otherwise would be glad to be at ease within modest bounds" must become acquisitive to survive. This is the central Hobbesian idea: that in a civilized, market-oriented society everyone must become materialistic if only to reduce one's vulnerability to aggression by others. The market *makes* people self-centred.

Two centuries later Karl Marx developed a more mature theory to explain the nature of intentional deterministic forces in the type of capitalistic system that had evolved to facilitate the realization of the *idea of progress*. His theory is global, for it examines both macro and micro implications within both a dynamic and a static framework. The major focus of subsequent scholars has been directed toward its macro-dynamic dimensions where, for example, there is a continuing debate as to whether the course of capitalist decay is determined by immutable scientific laws or whether the process can be deflected by the exercise of free will. However, our attention is directed towards the micro-static dimension where the basic statement is presented in the preface to *A Contribution to the Critique of Political Economy*.

I was led by my studies to the conclusion that legal relations as well as forms of the state ... are rooted in the material conditions of life ... In the social production which men carry on they enter into definite relations that are indispensable and independent of their will ... The sum total of these relations of production constitutes the economic structure of society ... to which correspond definite forms of social consciousness. The mode of production in material life *bedingt* the social, political and spiritual life processes *überhaupt*. (Marx 1913, 11)

Gouldner (1980) points out that the degree of determinism implied by the statement depends critically on whether *bedingt* is translated to mean "conditions" or "determines" and *überhaupt* is translated to mean "in general" or "altogether." But regardless of these nuances, there is no doubt about the general thrust of the statement.

Marx's observations about the impact of capitalistic structures on individual consciousness are spread throughout his work. One example is his discussion of the fetishism of commodities, a concept which "explores with brilliant suggestiveness the ramifications of the fact that men as social creatures are ruled not by intelligence or reason but by forces generated by their own handiwork in a commodity producing society" (Hook 1976, 5). For our purposes, Marx's line of reasoning can be reduced to four points:

- A commodity is not just an object with an exchange value but an embodiment of the social and technical relationships that exist amongst those involved in its production.
- In capitalism, the social relationship is characterized by the division of labour. This circumstance has led to the formation of a class structure in which capitalists extract surplus value from labour.
- Because of competition, the capitalist must seek to maximize output in order to ensure the survival of the productive unit and the maintenance of his position of dominance.
- Thus, the necessity of self-preservation engenders the accumulative drive among capitalists. This characteristic is transmitted to labour, who, lacking options and also interested in survival, must act in concert. That is, labour must adapt to the motions and rhythms required of it by capital and accept its acquisitive ethic, hardly aware that it is following the dictates of a social, not a natural, imperative. (See Heilbroner 1980, 117.)

Like Hobbes, Marx believed that many of the conditions of existence and the values embodied in *economic man* are determined by the economic system.

Marx's deterministic views are also revealed in his analysis of the alienation that arises within the specialized mode of production engendered by capitalism. In *The German Ideology* he and Engels state, "This fixation of social activity, this consolidation of what we ourselves produce into an objective power above us, growing out of our control, thwarting our expectations, bringing to naught our calculations, is one of the chief factors in historical development up till now" (Marx and Engels 1970, 53).

Until this century, the theories of Hobbes and Marx could only be considered to be plausible explanations of the impact of deterministic forces. This situation changed dramatically when controlled experimentation in the field of psychology revealed that in fact these forces shaped a significant portion of man's character. Of particular interest is the work of B.F. Skinner (1971), which led him to conclude that society could best be conceptualized as a network of operant conditioning mechanisms in which individuals respond to environmental stimuli in order to achieve pleasant states and avoid aversive ones. Some of these mechanisms are grounded in nature, but because of the increasing social complexity associated with fulfilment of the *idea of progress,* an increasing number are intentional. These intentional mechanisms can be either positive carrots or aversive sticks, and it is Skinner's insight (and Marx's oversight) that the essence of the civilizing process under capitalism is the substitution of positive for aversive techniques of control. Good grades replace the cane in the classroom; wage labour replaces slavery; conspicuous consumption replaces subsistence living. Society is more comfortable but not more free.

Skinner is very critical of social scientists who persist in attributing behaviour solely to noumenal forces. He argues that this practice has led to the false illusion that autonomous man exists and to the erection of a complex cultural superstructure based on that fallacy. One of the more pernicious aspects of this superstructure is that those who exert positive phenomenal force are absolved of responsibility for the course of events. Ironically, they are given credit for creating freedom when the opposite is the case, for as Rousseau observed, "There is no subjugation so perfect as that which keeps the appearance of freedom, for in that way one captures volition itself." To Skinner, we live in a world of costly deception. In the realm of action, we make ourselves vulnerable because we fail to understand the causes of events and our responses are correspondingly misguided. In the realm of ideas, pure noumenally based theory becomes increasingly irrelevant and, though enveloped in an aura of apparently benign mystification, increasingly counterproductive. One wonders why intellectuals have allowed this state of affairs to occur.

Hobbes, Marx, and Skinner have all attracted legions of supporters and critics, but the nuances of the various controversies need not concern us. What is significant is that there is sufficient plausibility to their theories to suggest that intentional phenomenal forces are an important determinant of behaviour and as such should be incorporated into any intellectual discipline that seeks to explain or predict human action. Orthodox economics fails to do so.

TECHNOLOGICAL THEORIES

The major thrust of this subset of theories is that the nature of technological development in industrial societies is such that the significance of intentional deterministic forces is increasing over time. Perhaps the most comprehensive analysis is that undertaken a generation ago by Jacques Ellul, who observed the increasing specialization and regimentation in the workplace, the demand for orderly lifestyles, and the emphasis on careers as the mode of personal fulfilment. He concluded that "technology has monopolized all human forces, passions, intelligences and virtues" in such a way that freedom and independence, as conceptualized in orthodox circles, had become a fiction. He stated,

Technique can never engender freedom. Of course, Technique frees mankind from a whole collection of ancient constraints. It is evident, for example, that it liberates him from the limits imposed on him by time and space; that man, through its agency, is free (or at least tending to become free) from famine, excessive heat and cold, the rhythms of the seasons, and from the gloom of night; that the race is freed from certain social constraints through its commerce with the universe, and from its intellectual limitations through its accumulation of information. But is this what it means really to be free? Other constraints as oppressive and rigorous as the traditional ones are imposed on the human being in today's technological society through the agency of Technique. New limits and technical oppressions have taken the place of the older, natural constraints, and we certainly cannot aver that much has been gained. The problem is deeper – the operation of Technique is the contrary of freedom, an operation of determinism and necessity. Technique is an ensemble of rational and efficient practices; a collection of orders, schemes, and mechanisms. All of this expresses very well a necessary order and a determinate process, but one into which freedom, unorthodoxy, and the sphere of the gratuitous and spontaneous cannot penetrate. All that these last could possibly introduce is discord and disorder. The more technical actions increase in society, the more human autonomy and initiative diminish. The more the human being comes to exist in a world of ever increasing demands (fortified with technical apparatus possessing its own laws to meet these demands), the more he loses any possibility of free choice and individuality in action. (Ellul 1979, 18)

Ellul's conclusion is supported by Marshall McLuhan's (1969) theories about the electronic media. He argued that the media reworks the ratio of man's senses, numbing some and extending others, so that one perceives reality, formulates values, and acts through the filter of an altered sensory state. In turn, the media is adapted to satisfy the demands of this new being, so that the two become engaged in a process of mutual reinforcement and dependency. Man and machine simultaneously become appendages, both incapable of independent action.

John Kenneth Galbraith (1967) has explored another implication of the rush toward technological sophistication. He observed that the tendency toward capital-intensive methods has a direct visible effect on the structure of industry and, as well, an indirect, but ubiquitous, effect on individual behaviour. That is, capital intensity leads to corporate concentration, long gestation periods, and inflexible production processes. As planning horizons lengthen, industrial decision makers become increasingly concerned about stability and initiate policies to minimize the possibility of surprise. Governments are persuaded to absorb the economic shocks that would otherwise destabilize the macro system; competition is eliminated through mergers and collusion; negative externalities are addressed through the creation of adjunct capital-intensive technologies; preference shaping becomes the responsibility of a corporatist communications industry. These forces create a servile population, dependent on government for stability, on corporations for jobs and goods, and on technology for comfort and safety. Consumerism becomes a creed and non-conformity becomes an anathema. The magic of the system is the simultaneous creation and satisfaction of wants, and in the end the consumer sovereignty of the textbooks is replaced in the real world by producer sovereignty. To quote Galbraith, "The imperatives of technology and organization, not the images of ideology are what determines the shape of economic society" (Galbraith 1967, 19). Roszak (1979) has added a disturbing footnote to this analysis by pointing out that the complexity of many large industrial units often exceeds the intellectual capacity of those who man them. Under these circumstances, systems are driven by their own momentum and can continue to shape both public attitudes and public policy to suit their own programs, immune from human attempts to deflect them. Man is slowly imprisoned by his own handiwork.

In short, there are many reasons to believe that deterministic forces originating in the technological system are becoming more pervasive over time: regimentation and orderliness are standard aspects of behaviour; economic power is more concentrated, as are the resources necessary to shape public attitudes; consumer sovereignty is withering; the media continues to develop more sophisticated preference-shaping techniques. Determinism is becoming increasingly ubiquitous, symbiotic, and effective.

EROSION THEORIES

The technological apparatus that provides the means for actualizing the *idea of progress* not only generates its own deterministic forces, it also erodes those aspects of the social arrangement that strengthen man's capacity to exercise free will. That is, the phenomenal attacks and weakens the noumenal.

This line of reasoning is predicated on the idea that there are two different modes of cognition, the scientific-objective and the emotive-subjective, and that wisdom requires that they be merged into a synthesis of rationalism and spiritualism. (One of the more comprehensive artistic statements of this concept is in Wagner's *Ring des Nibelungen* operas. See Donington 1963.) Further, since wisdom is seen as a prerequisite for attaining freedom, anything that disrupts this synthesis is debilitating. Given this, the aggressiveness of technical phenomena on the noumena is seen to be focused on changing the relative potency of different institutions and attributes in order to elevate the rational and suppress the spiritual. Hence it diminishes the possibility that freedom can be attained.

The issue can be examined by looking at the impact of technology and the *idea of progress* on particular institutions that traditionally strengthen man's noumenal character. In Western society, this approach invariably leads to a discussion of the extent to which secularization has eroded religion. As man places more confidence in scientific understanding and as mystical explanations of events seem less plausible, the need for faith in the divine seems to recede as does the necessity for making moral choices, which is the very essence of freedom. Secularism shrinks the psyche.

Many religious philosophers have addressed this deprival. For example, Cox (1969) has analysed the role of religious festivals and fantasies in Western history. In the pre-industrial era, festivals celebrated historical events and gave comfort to celebrants who, through spiritual association with their roots, saw themselves within the spectrum of their ancestry. Similarly, fantasy permitted the metaphysical creation of imaginary worlds of goodness and justice and the hope that they might some day be realized.

In industrial societies, festivals and fantasies take on different forms. The temporal focus shifts to the present and the societal focus collapses into egocentricity and nuclear family bonding. Festivals become times for display and excess; fantasy is directed toward personal achievement rather than to issues of cosmic destiny. That is, the *idea of progress* has infiltrated these practices and transformed them. Whereas they were previously religious forces contributing to wisdom and freedom, they are now elements in the individualistic superstructure of capitalism.

A second institution traditionally charged with the responsibility of maintaining the will to acquire wisdom and freedom is the educational system. Technology also erodes this system's ability to fulfil its mandate. One avenue is by direct penetration of the curriculum and the pedagogy. For example, Roszak (1986) argues that the increasing use of the computer in schools diminishes its effectiveness as a force for freedom because the intellectual skills of users are directed toward rational information processing rather than criticism, creativity, and value formation. Gouldner (1976) has examined another way in which technology has diminished the effectiveness of formal education. He distinguishes between a society's cultural apparatus – schools, the theatre, museums – and its consciousness industry – television, popular music, and so on. Technological advance is concentrated in the latter, primarily because of the profit motive, so that it is now the more effective source of information and ideas. Its transmission systems harmonize with the perceived needs of a dynamic ecocentric society; its marketing networks monitor consumer behaviour and reinforce those patterns that contribute to the industry's commercial objectives. As the cultural apparatus in general and the public education system in particular diminish in influence, so also does the freedom of the citizenry because they have lost access to the types of information and the forms of contemplation and criticism that are prerequisites for its realization.

The thrust of what have been referred to as technological and erosion theories has been skilfully co-ordinated in George Grant's (1986) response to the proposition that "the computer does not impose on us the ways in which it should be used." Generally, orthodox economists will agree with the statement. However, Grant dissects it into its constituent phrases and reaches an alternative conclusion.

To Grant the phrase "the computer does not impose" is misleading because it obscures what the machine really is: a representation of a particular paradigm of knowledge. In fact, use of the computer imposes that paradigm and its destiny as well. The phrase "the ways" is also misleading. Computers with their huge capacity for storage and retrieval open up vistas of analysis that are not otherwise available. Furthermore, they can only be built and operated in societies that have large institutions and are likely to be attuned to the value system and power structure in those societies. Finally, the word "should" conveys a normative meaning and hence the definition of good and bad that is consistent with the prevailing world-view. For these reasons, Grant disputes the veracity of the statement. He concludes,

When we represent technology to ourselves as an array of neutral instruments, invented by human beings and under human control, we are expressing a kind of common sense, but it is a common sense seen from within the very technology we are attempting to represent ... We are led to forget that the modern destiny [i.e., the *idea of progress*] permeates our representation of the world and ourselves ... It is a destiny which enfolds us in its own conceptions of instrumentality, neutrality and purposiveness. It is in this sense that it has been truthfully said: technology is the ontology of the age. (Grant 1986, 32)

In other words, the forces of determinism are such that man is only free to behave within the strictures and definitions inherent in the *idea of progress* and its technological apparatus. He *must* behave like *economic man*.

THE IMPLICATIONS

If intentional deterministic forces are influencing the motivations and behaviour of the citizens of Western societies, it follows that intellectual disciplines concerned with the human condition in these societies should recognize the existence of these forces within their analytical domains. The paradigm of orthodox economics should be modified accordingly.

For this change to be accomplished, it will be necessary to alter treatment of the underlying premise about man's character. Currently, his noumenal features are captured in the *economic man* axiom. However, this principle will have to be augmented by the inclusion of his phenomenal attributes as an *output* of economic processes. Two comments seem appropriate. First, if man is to be treated simultaneously as an axiom and an outcome, an element of circularity is introduced into economic theory. However, this factor will not create overwhelming methodological problems. There are examples of circularity in existing orthodox theory (e.g., multiplier-accelerator or monopoly profit-innovation models) and what is proposed is merely another situation in which an antecedent state is modified by an economic process to become an altered state. Second, one might contemplate the suitability of retaining *economic man* in a dual role of axiom and output within a positivistic framework. However, this approach would be sub-optimal. If human characteristics are outputs of economic processes, they need to be evaluated, so that in effect the discipline must become normative. Further, as *economic man* has been shown to be normatively inferior, largely because his freedom is constrained by his own technology, he is expunged within an optimizing paradigm. One way to resolve the dilemma is to construct a new paradigm that incorporates a more normatively satisfying conceptualization of phenomenal man as the desired outcome of economic activity.

This solution opens up a huge vista of possibilities. For example, what is the new conceptualization to be? What are the implications if the change forces economics into a paradigm based on gestalt, rather than pure, theory? Does the change take economics outside the *idea of progress* and does it cease to become an advocate of capitalism? These questions will be addressed presently, but for now it is convenient to summarize the line of reasoning presented so far in the form of the following proposition:

Proposition 1. Technologically induced phenomenal forces are an increasingly significant output of our industrial system. The economics discipline should incorporate this fact into its analytical domain and evaluate it accordingly. This approach transforms economics into a normative field of inquiry, in which case, the inferiority of *economic man* is revealed, as is the need to introduce a more normatively satisfactory conceptualization of the human condition into the domain.

It would be naïve to underestimate the magnitude of the change that is being advocated. Therefore it is prudent to pause and reflect about the likelihood that reform is possible. In doing so, it is resourceful to cast the net widely and inquire about the responses of other intellectual disciplines when their axiomatic structure has been challenged. There is nothing the matter with learning by analogy: Adam Smith used the model of Newtonian physics to establish the basis of orthodoxy; it is reasonable to use the experiences of other disciplines as guidelines when seeking to effect the reform of economics.

Examination of this issue reveals that there is a substantial literature on the very question we seek to address. One of the scholars who has contributed most to this field is Michel Foucault, and it is instructive to review his ideas.

THE FOUCAULT REMEDY

Foucault's work defies categorization within traditional disciplinary boundaries. He reached intellectual maturity during a period of time when there was intense controversy among French structuralists, Marxists, and existentialists about how orthodox social sciences and humanities disciplines should best be reformed so as to make them conform more accurately with real social processes. The central theme of structuralism is that beneath the surface of human rationality there is not only a morass of irrationality (as revealed by psychologists such as Freud and Jung) but an even deeper level of linguistically related rationality which provides the foundation of meaningful existence. For Marxists, society can best be understood by interpreting it in terms of underlying forces such as the mode of production, commodity fetishism, class conflict, and alienation. For existentialists, human fulfilment requires that one see through the surface of rationality and restrictive institutions and deal directly with the anxiety that is a natural condition of existence. In spite of their obvious differences, these movements shared the belief that one can only understand social processes and institutions by probing beneath the veneer of surface appearances. Although Foucault did not identify directly with any of the three protagonist schools, he patterned his own research program so as to be similarly penetrative.

When he applied this principle to orthodox intellectual disciplines, he concluded that they could best be understood as *nodes of power* and that their behaviour, direction, strengths, and vulnerabilities should be interpreted accordingly. His intellectual mentor in this formulation was undoubtedly Nietzsche, and it is useful to digress briefly to discuss this eminent and controversial philosopher because many of his ideas are relevant to us.

Friedrich Nietzsche is often regarded as the master iconoclast of the nineteenth century for he attacked virtually every aspect of conventional wisdom with a barrage of insightful aphorisms. His influence, while not immediate, was ubiquitous and helped to shape such diverse movements as existentialism and Naziism. He remains controversial, partly because his vanity led him to believe that he did not have to support his ideas with logical argumentation and partly because in his later years he degenerated from brilliance into madness. Consequently, interpreters of his work are often left in a quandary as to whether they are reading drivel, flashes of genius emanating from a disturbed mind, or part of some elegant scheme of thought that is only comprehensible to someone with superior intelligence. These issues continue to be debated.

However, there is no debate about the intensity of his passion, for he vigorously attacked all three of the intellectual movements that dominated his age: rationalism, idealism, and humanism. His position has been summarized as follows:

[Nietzsche believed that] Western thinkers immersed in the high problems of philosophy had gone astray in three ways. Materialistic or empirical rationalists ... had falsified and suppressed full human experience by erecting the dream-world we now call science. Idealistic rationalists ... had achieved a similar falsification and suppression by erecting the even more fantastic dream-world of idealism, [the world of] Kant and Hegel. Finally, gross men miscalled artists ... had tried to do without these intellectual dream-worlds, and had fallen back on their "doggish lusts" and sentimental memories as guides to conduct. (Brinton 1965, 97)

Nietzsche deplored the lack of realism in each of these movements, arguing that they ignore the real tyrannies and opportunities of existence. They waste their energies searching for some single eternal truth that could guide behaviour. In Christianity it is the search for the one true god and in rationalism it is the search for the single, completely true body of natural law. However, such quests are misguided because they result in repression. Christianity's moral imperatives impose a force that inhibits individual fulfilment and precludes experimentation to the point where repression of the self had become the primary characteristic of Western civilization; rationalism precludes reflection and the search for the reality that underlies both reason and unreason.

Nietzsche took on the task of explaining how this state of affairs had arisen. His conclusion was that it can be understood if one conceptualizes reality in terms of interacting power relationships. In fact, Nietzsche saw power as the unifying force that keeps society together, in much the same way that Newton saw gravitation as the force that keeps the solar system together and Smith saw the invisible hand as the force that keeps the economic system together.

The motivation to achieve power originates within each individual's mind from an imperfectly harmonized array of "will points" that guide behaviour. Thus driven, a person does not struggle to survive so much as he or she survives to struggle for increased power. There are, of course, individual differences in both the intensity of this will and the skill with which power is pursued.

This way of thinking led Nietzsche to support the "great man" theory of history, which is based on the proposition that society is moulded by a few individuals who obtain great personal power and have lasting influence. In itself, this observation is neither profound nor original; however, a Nietzschean corollary was to cause great controversy. This was the idea that throughout history there seemed to be two different types of individuals who achieve power, as symbolized by warriors and priests.

It is convenient to think of these two categories as Weberian "ideal types." The warrior is open in his exercise of power and abhors compromise, exhaustion, or defeat. He is strong, zestful, and driven by the sense of honour and intellectual integrity rather than self-interest. He is patterned after Dionysus, a god of joy, turbulence, and panache, as represented by Homeric heroes in ancient Greece and by Zorba in contemporary Greece. Alternatively, the priest is physically weak but attains power through stealth and manipulation. He solidifies his power by oratory and calls for temperance and moderation. He neutralizes the warrior by preaching about the merit of an Apollonian philosophy of life in which one should search for harmony and the golden mean of Socrates rather than use one's creative juices.

Nietzsche believed that one of the distinguishing characteristics of modern society is that priests repeatedly overpower warriors by gaining the support of the populace through persuasive, but devious, oratory. This proposition has many fascinating implications. For example, it suggests that we must not be mesmerized by the apparent wisdom of self-proclaimed learned men because very often their pronouncements are designed more to extend their own power than to reveal truth. Another implication is that, contrary to Darwin and Spenser, society may be turning out weaker, rather than stronger, men and that if we are to transcend mediocrity, Dionysian servants must rebel against their Apollonian masters and create a "transvaluation of values."

These various insights triggered an explosion of philosophical inquiry. Among the many scholars who built an intellectual edifice on Nietzschean foundations was Foucault; his particular focus of concern was the behaviour of the priests within contemporary intellectual disciplines.

There are three Nietzschean threads running through Foucault's work that are particularly relevant. The first is that society can be conceptualized as a set of interacting *power relationships*. The second is the idea that, while reward and repression can still be effective methods of exercising power, another force has now achieved primacy. This is self-subjugation or *discipline*, which is particularly effective in capitalist societies because it can be imposed without destroying the illusion of freedom. (This idea is a variation on Skinner's positive conditioners theme.) The third, and for our purposes most important, thread is the idea that in recent history, the distribution of power has been shaped by self-serving priests in orthodox intellectual disciplines who are primarily concerned with enhancing their own power as oracles, and do so by a particular device: they corrupt the truth to create *knowledge* that is then dispensed to the citizenry until it is accepted as conventional wisdom. This then becomes the lens through which reality is interpreted and public policy decisions are formulated.

I propose to review each of these ideas briefly to provide a basis for explaining Foucault's strategy for reforming errant intellectual disciplines. Foucault believes that *power relationships* permeate all aspects of human existence. He states, "When I think of the mechanics of power, I think of its capillary form of existence, of the extent to which power seeps into the very grain of individuals, reaches right into their bodies, permeates their gestures, their posture, what they say, how they learn to live and work with other people." (See Sheridan 1980, 217.)

To substantiate his view, he undertakes detailed studies of specific power networks in society. Of particular relevance is his analysis of the helping professions (e.g., medicine, psychology, psychiatry, the clergy, the police, and the judiciary) and his conclusion that in each realm there is a coalition between professionals and academics, who, while explaining their collective actions as manifestations of their humane concern, are primarily interested in their own aggrandizement.

It is interesting to apply this perspective to the economic system, where it would seem that the coalition is bonded by its common focus on issues related to the creation and distribution of money. Power is concentrated in the hands of the captains of industry and government, with economists acting as oracles. In the public arena, they advise government about taxation, expenditure, and regulatory policies, and about issues related to central banking and deficit financing. When these recommendations are implemented, the citizenry is usually co-opted into compliance and effectively disenfranchised. For example, in the case of deficit financing, the primary role of money changes from being a simple lubricant to become part of an elaborate system of credit in which the state extracts money from savers in exchange for debt instruments, thereby creating two mutually reinforcing tenacles of power. First, the state has even more money to distribute. Second, the holders of the debt instruments are obliged to support the continuation of the state apparatus if they expect to be repaid. Thus the lender is trapped because his own money is used to secure his loyalty to the existing system of authority.

Very often corporations become involved with these coalitions, providing additional complexity to the nodes and additional barriers to their penetration by the citizenry. As earlier noted, Galbraith (1967) cites contemporary examples; Polanyi (1944) describes some of their historical antecedents. In the latter case, nineteenth-century European governments are shown to have collaborated with *haut finance* to borrow massive amounts on international money markets. When their profits and power required peace, there was peace; when they required war, there was war. In all situations, the saving citizen was the victim, either as a supplier of funds or a soldier in the trenches. There are also cases from Canadian economic history of the use of money to attain power through dual entrapment. For example, the granting of franchises to organizations such as the Canadian Pacific Railway and the flotation of government bonds to assist in their financing inflicted on Canadians the obligation to support the continuance of this type of monopolistic organization.

However, to identify these economic liaisons and the nuances of the saving process is only to see the tip of the money-power iceberg. It is a ubiquitous, hierarchical network. In reality, most daily life experiences are conditioned by the availability of money: breadwinners control families, employers control workers, audiences control performers, and so on. It is a force from which the individual cannot escape. One of Orwell's characters describes the extent to which it penetrates the consciousness, even of those who live in poverty. "The money-god is so cunning. If he only baited his traps with yachts and race-horses, tarts and champagne, how easy it would be to dodge him. It is when he gets at you through your sense of decency that he finds you helpless" (Orwell 1966, 246).

In short, if one conceptualizes the economic system as a network of power centres and money as the means by which they are entrenched, the role of the economist – both in the academies and elsewhere – is seen in a refracted light. When, say, he is involved in trying to design a fiscal system that facilitates efficient growth, he is simultaneously supporting a particular power regime. Hence his activities are not ideologically neutral, in spite of any positivistic protestations to the contrary.

The second thread of Foucault's analysis is his identification of *discipline* or self-subjugation as the force that is the primary mechanism for exercising power in contemporary society. In conjunction with its two more visible companion mechanisms, reward and repression, discipline effectively controls the citizenry in such a way that its behaviour is supportive of existing regimes. Foucault suggests that discipline is less visible because we have misunderstood the origins of the *idea of progress*. We tend to think that the idea was initiated by philosophers when, in fact, it also has military roots. He states,

Historians of ideas usually attribute the dream of a perfect society to the philosophers and jurists of the eighteenth century; but there was also a military dream of society; its fundamental reference was not to the state of nature, but to the meticulously subordinated cogs of a machine, not to the primal social contract, but to permanent coercions, not to fundamental rights, but to indefinitely progressive forms of training, not to the general will, but to automatic docility. (Foucault 1979, 169)

Militaristic discipline became particularly effective when the spread of industrialism spawned factories and eventually corporations and bureaucracies. Large numbers of men and women needed to be co-ordinated efficiently so chains of command, clearly defined responsibilities, regimentation of time, and logistical patterns became commonplace. Unquestionably, the primary beneficiaries of these disciplinary practices are those in positions of authority.

There are several reasons why discipline is an effective mechanism for exercising economic power. It is marvelously efficient because, unlike systems of reward and repression, it does not require expenditures for surveillance, monitoring, enforcement, or punishment. Furthermore, discipline in the economic realm is supported by complementary practices in other institutions (e.g., schools, hospitals, public agencies, churches, and households) so that the conditioning task is shared and mutually reinforcing. Indeed, discipline is the very essence of two of the most fundamental attitudes in Western society: self-denial and self-realization. The former is the ubiquitous basis of our religious heritage, and as Freud observed, "It is impossible to overlook the extent to which civilization is built on the renunciation of instinct." Its partner, self-realization, requires a similar degree of self-imposed suppression. Discipline is the means by which this renunciation is actualized, but the indirect beneficiaries of these apparently voluntary practices are those with privilege.

An additional factor that strengthens the role of discipline in the economic arena is the erection of an effective protective shield. This is the practice of "normalization" through the identification of accepted codes of behaviour with respect to such things as etiquette, dress, speech, sexuality, and political practices. Most think of these standards as desirable manifestations of civility and progress; to Foucault they are features on the Dorian Gray face of entrenched power that are designed to foster compliance. Furthermore, once normal is defined, so also is its opposite, deviance. In a series of detailed studies, he suggests that the practices developed to deal with deviants are not directed toward cure or reform but rather toward isolation and, as such, strengthen the forces of conformity and engender respect for the normal.

Thus, because *discipline* is efficient, exercised across a broad spectrum of institutions, and protected by the practice of normalization, it has become the most effective mechanism of power in the contemporary world. To Foucault, it is "one of the great inventions of bourgeois society."

Given this understanding of *power relationships* as the forces that bind society together and of *discipline* as the primary mechanism of control, we can now turn to the third Nietzschean thread of Foucault's work and undertake a more detailed examination of the role of intellectual disciplines such as orthodox economics.

If one looks at the broad sweep of history, academia has always been organized around the existing power structure. In pre-industrial societies, power resided with the church and the aristocracy, and universities had a compatible focus, developing centres to study issues that appealed to the tastes of these groups. With industrialization, urbanization, social complexity, and technological innovation, the power nodes in society were dispersed and became specialized. Universities followed a similar path as they became internally fragmented and developed specialized disciplines to study each node in detail. It was in this context that orthodox economics emerged.

Ironically, the discipline's current theoretical orientation precludes the possibility that it can accurately perceive the realities of society's power network. Purity demands that links to nodes outside the domain be severed, and in the absence of comprehensiveness, comprehension becomes problematic; furthermore, quantification eliminates the possibility of studying *discipline* as a mechanism and the many nuances and subtleties of its exercise. Orthodoxy is only able to treat power in very simple terms, as when money is superficially equated with buying power. By failing to address its complexity, economics condones its abuses.

In fact, the orthodox discipline indirectly supports the existing power structure with great vigour. Its claim to be positive rather than normative signals a non-critical attitude about exploitation; its emphasis on efficiency in the workplace encourages behavioural patterns that generate extractable surplus; its argument that non-market externalities can be handled most efficiently by the public sector provides a rationale for the expansion of government; its harmony axiom discourages social disruption amongst the disadvantaged; and as indicated, the fact that it ignores *discipline* as a mechanism of power legitimizes its use. However, orthodoxy's most incisive blow in support of the existing power regime is probably a consequence of the central role it attaches to private investment as the engine of progress. Capital-intensive investment is seen as a panacea because it increases labour productivity, provides opportunities for scale economies, and facilitates innovation. Not surprising the primary beneficiaries of this orientation are those who have the greatest access to investment funds: the monopoly capitalists. Once this class is entrenched, the power of the state is also enhanced as it expands to provide the supportive infrastructure and the systems necessary to ameliorate the adverse externalities caused by these production techniques.

These observations reinforce the notion that orthodox economics is an ideology rather than a positive science. It is able to cloud the distinction by skilful definition and manipulation of its paradigmatic structure. Of the infinite number of variables in the gestalt world, it selects a subset for inclusion in its pure domain of analysis, attaches arbitrary significance to selected variables within this domain, and then analyses their interaction scientifically. Foucault terms the results of such exercises *knowledge* as distinct from *truth*.

With this perspective about orthodoxy, let us return to the original inquiry about the implications of introducing phenomenal forces into the orthodox paradigm as well as replacing the *economic man* axiom with something more normatively satisfying (Proposition 1). Our excursion into Foucault's work teaches us that the task is more formidable than might have previously appeared. *Economic man* has served the power system very well, and there is bound to be resistance to suggestions that he be discarded. Furthermore, as power is a ubiquitous network of mutually reinforcing nodes, resistance will also be ubiquitous. Finally, because one is challenging knowledge rather than truth, one's avenues of argumentation are correspondingly limited.

Nevertheless the excursion has been enlightening because, if orthodoxy is an ideology that covertly supports a questionable power regime, integrity requires that it be challenged. Furthermore, Foucault has proposed a general principle that can act as a procedural guideline. In a 1976 lecture (Gordon 1980) he describes a technique "whose validity is not dependent on the approval of established regimes of thought" but rather on gestalt truth. It is based on the awareness that there are a variety of subjugated knowledges which have been buried and disguised by the orthodox social sciences. These knowledges or sub-sets of truth have been relegated to an inferior status, not because they are dormant in the human mind or because they are insignificant motivators of behaviour, but rather because they are below the required level of scientism. They do not represent ignorance and misinformation, but nevertheless they are treated as an underclass or as "the deviants of the knowledge species."

Foucault argues that these subjugated knowledges fall into two general classes: universal and local. The former relates to the overriding principles of human endeavour and the latter to individual experiences as confined in time and space. If the truth is to be discovered, these categories should be combined in an "insurrection of subjugated knowledges" to confront intellectual orthodoxy. If applied to our own task, this approach means that the alternative to *economic man* should include elements of both the universal and the local. In the next two chapters I will be more specific about what the process entails, but for reference purposes it is convenient to identify it as Proposition 2.

Proposition 2.   In operationalizing Proposition 1, the more normatively satisfying axiom about the human condition that is to replace *economic man* should include elements of both universal and local knowledge.

3 Universal Knowledge

The fear and the celebration of the unknown
is the beginning of wisdom.

The previous chapter suggested that the best way to confront a flawed intellectual discipline such as orthodox economics is to challenge it with a coalition of universal and local knowledges, which are woven together to create a new vantage point from which reality can be perceived. The task in this chapter is to formulate an hypothesis concerning the nature of universal knowledge. Given that my line of inquiry was initiated by the desire to articulate a definition of human potentiality that is more normatively satisfying than that which is embodied by *economic man*, I interpret this task to be one of identifying conditions that will enhance Western man's existence.

Man embeds his definitions of meaningfulness and fulfilment in his myths, a collection of popular, historically rooted narratives that present principles of existence, even when they are not literally true. There is a spectrum of mythical types. At one extreme are vulgar folktales, which are retained in the culture to entertain and to alert us to life's ironies. At the other, myths can be sacred stories that have great symbolic significance as behavioural guidelines. It is this latter category that is of interest.

The primary source of sacred myths in Western society is the Bible. It teaches us to juxtapose time and space; it provides us with unifying symbols and rituals; it outlines codes for self and community behaviour; it points to remedies for resolving conflicts; it strikes a balance between illusion and reality so as to provide a framework for both intellectual inquiry and emotional fulfilment.

Frye (1981) has demonstrated that in spite of its rich diversity, the Bible has a single, primary theme: the myth of deliverance, according to which man periodically falls into bondage in an alien world but is rescued by individual commitment and/or community action. Further, he shows that the Bible can be viewed as a sequence of surprisingly similar stories having a common narrative structure that is "roughly U-shaped, the apostasy being followed by a descent into disaster and bondage, which in turn is followed by repentance then a rise through deliverance to a point more or less on the level from which the descent began" (171). The myth is repeated over and over, but stories of Moses and Jesus have become the archetypes for the Old and New Testaments.

For the past twenty centuries humanists have sought to reinterpret the myth of deliverance in the context of the specific forms of bondage being experienced in their own times. Of special interest are those who have expressed the view that we human beings are being imprisoned by the *idea of progress* and have sought means whereby we might extricate ourselves. While they constitute a long list, there are three who are felt to be particularly insightful and whose ideas can be co-ordinated into a coherent interpretation of universal knowledge. These three are William Blake, Søren Kierkegaard, and Paul Tillich.

THE INTELLECTUAL ROOTS

Blake was a poet-artist-visionary who lived during the early stages of the industrial revolution and who detected gross imperfections in the world around him. He was particularly bitter about the dominance of rationalism and the tendency of organized religion to postulate a vengeful god. These factors seemed to be impediments to the realization of the human potential because they result in the misallocation and repression of human energy. Blake's art juxtaposes this reality against his ideas about the conditions necessary for human fulfilment and thereby points out the path that man must follow if he is to transcend the banal and achieve enlightenment.

The essence of the argument is presented in his *Book of Urizen* and *Jerusalem*, where he provides a biblically based interpretation of human history. Initially, in eternity or Eden, mankind is undivided and fulfilled. Men and women, body and soul, man and God, and man's energies or Zoas (reason, passion, sensation, and instinct) exist as one entity, exemplified best by the spirit of Christ. But mankind falls and the unity is shattered. Men begin to dominate women, the body dominates the spirit, the joyousness of God is suppressed, and reason is elevated over the other energies. What follows is an epoch in which prudence, wisdom, and morality are redefined and in which there is descent from the opportunity of Christ to the vanity of institutionalized religion, adherence to dogma and analytical reason, and the evolution of an imprisoned mind. Blake is particularly distressed by the continuing elevation of reason, arguing that Christ should be man's model and that he "was all virtue, and acted from impulse not from rules" (Ostriker 1977, 193).

To Blake, the industrial revolution and the *idea of progress* are contemporary manifestations of our descent. To deliver ourselves from these tyrannies, we must resituate the divine and recognize the immanence of God. But this process can only be accomplished imaginatively, for that is where divinity is centred. That is, in contradistinction to Descartes and Newton, who thought that God was revealed through the patterns of nature, Blake's search was introspective. Given this, it is understandable that he had antipathy toward the orthodox religions of the day, which postulated that God is an all-seeing, anthropomorphic, external reality who instructs and judges mankind, rewarding us for virtue and punishing us for transgression.

Once one correctly locates the seat of divinity, transcendence is possible. It occurs when, given the existence of sense data, imagination is synthesized with reason to reveal new vistas of understanding. This blossoming is captured in the statements "Man's perceptions are not bounded by organs of perception. He perceives more than sense can discover ... He who sees the infinite in all things, sees God. He who sees the ratio only, sees himself only" (Ostriker 1977, 75–6). Furthermore, when divinely inspired imagination is brought to bear on one's energies, they are reintegrated and the unity that was lost in the fall is reacquired.

Before proceeding, it is prudent to pause and to note that once one invokes the diety as an element that should influence human action, one necessarily incorporates the unknown and the unknowable into the analysis. In the previous chapter it was observed that Descartes, Newton, and Locke all sought to ground their theories in God and were required ultimately to construct unproven and unprovable axioms (e.g., that God is not a deceiving God; that God created a harmonious, mechanistic system; that there is a hierarchy amongst the species) to buttress a pure theory. In contrast, Blake retains the unproven and unprovable within a gestalt theoretical scheme. Thus it seems that regardless of whether the unknown aspects of the divine are assigned to the generic axioms that confine a theory or retained as variables within the theory itself, they continue to exist.

That is to say, the divine is a component of all theories, and while it can be obscured by scientific terminology, it cannot be eliminated.

In any case, there are fascinating methodological implications arising from Blake's desire to place divinity at the center of his theoretical stage. Specifically, the idea that transcendence is only possible through the interpenetration of imagination and reason forces one to juxtapose attributes that are normally considered to be contraries and hold them in a tense union. Perhaps the most explicit statement of this insight is in *The Marriage of Heaven and Hell*, which is generally recognized as Blake's first full-scale attack on orthodoxy and an exuberant declaration of his own principles.

In *The Marriage of Heaven and Hell* the *idea of progress* is condemned because it isolates and suppresses certain of the creative energies that can lead man to godliness. Salvation is accomplished by counter-manding suppression and reunifying the seemingly contrary Zoas. The focus of the poem is captured in the statements "Without Con-traries is no progression. Attraction and Repulsion, Reason and Energy, Love and Hate, are necessary to Human existence." These words are followed by a series of aphorisms, including some that show disdain for orthodoxy's repressive morality – "Prudence is a rich ugly old maid courted by Incapacity ... As the catterpillar chooses the fairest leaves to lay her eggs on, so the priest lays his curse on the fairest joys" – and some that celebrate energy and freedom: "No bird soars too high if he soars with his own wings ... You never know what is enough unless you know what is more than enough" (Ostriker 1977, 181–5). Blake envisions a new world order arising from the union of contraries.

What is coming is the union of heat and light, a marriage of heaven and hell. By "hell" Blake means an upsurge of desire and passion ... so great that it will destroy the present starry [orthodox] heaven, and he calls it "hell" because that is what the orthodox call it. (Frye 1947, 197)

It seems that a fundamental error of the *idea of progress* is that it defines as evil the very attributes that are essential for fulfilment! Blake and others (e.g., Kazantzakis 1957) point out that the Christian message is that Jesus was able to achieve salvation by unifying con-traries; giants of scholarship such as Jung and Wagner have developed similar themes concerning secular affairs. It is an idea of immense methodological and practical significance.

A second methodological implication of Blake's scheme is that ques-tions of ultimate ends are answered by his dynamics, in which, optimally, a continuous tension is created between a receding potential and an improving actuality. That is, as man begins to transcend his banality and take on the image of God, his awareness of his potential is similarly elevated. To quote one Blakean scholar, "Man attains his own divinity, not by making over his agential status to a god figure but by a continuing tension, a continuing awareness that his divinity is only projected, a potential which must be measured against reality" (Punter 1982, 101). The idea of dynamic intersecting tensions – between imagination and reason and between actual and potential – is central to Blake's theory and to the concept of universal knowledge that I seek to define. The essential point is that the contraries must be held in a symbiotic unity devoid of domination. That is, Blake is not asking that imagination replace reason but that the two be accorded equivalence. His lament about the era in which he lived is that reason had become too dominant. Man had severed part of his own psyche, objectified it, and given it independent authenticity. He had constructed a religious system based on dogmatism, an economic system based on greed, and a distribution system based on inequality. A divine-seeking imagination must enter fully into man's thought processes if this situation is to be rectified. In spite of detractors, Blake is optimistic that transcendence can occur at the national level. In *Jerusalem: The Emanation of the Giant Albion* he prophesied a "Jerusalem in England's green and pleasant land." A modern critic has made the following comment about this poem.

Albion is the collective being of the English nation. He is England. He is the sleeping lord who has fallen into the deadly sleep of materialism ... The dark satanic mills, the enslavement of women and children to the machines, the conscription of the young men into the armies to fight in Europe, all these things which Blake indicates were the deeds of Albion in his alienation of the divine within him. Blake believed that Albion could be awakened, that it was the task of the [humanists]. Blake believed it would happen. (CBC 1987, 17)

There is a sleeping Albion in all industrial nations. Canada is no exception.

There is also a direct economic implication in Blake's new Jerusalem because work takes on dimensions that are only dimly recognized in the industrial age. It ceases to be viewed as an arduous means of obtaining commodities but instead becomes a celebration of energy contributing to transcendence. Man produces according to what is commonly referred to as value in use rather than value in exchange, learns that work gives him a grasp of natural and community forces, and sees it as a means of expressing humane qualities. "The stones are pity, and the bricks, well wrought affections: / Enameled with love & kindness, & the tiles engraven gold / Labor of merciful hands: the beams & rafters are forgiveness: / The mortar and cement of the work, tears of honesty "(Ostriker 1977, 655).

Blake's theme about the divergence between the potential of work and its depressing actuality has also persisted to the present. (See, for example, Veblen 1900 and Schumacher 1973.) One of the more interesting contemporary statements is the Papal Encyclical of 1981, *Laborem Exercens*, where Blake's shadow is very visible and accompanied by a plethora of biblical references. The following sentences summarize the thrust of its argument. "In the modern period, Christian truth about work had to oppose the various trends of materialistic and economistic thought ... Man is treated as an instrument of production, whereas he ought to be treated as the effective subject of work and its true maker and creator ... This spirituality of work should be a heritage shared by all ... In the final analysis it is always man who is the purpose of work" (John Paul II 1981, 23, 25, 88, 23). Many who are embedded in the *idea of progress* paradigm probably find Blake's views and those of the Catholic Church to be impractical. However, there is a nation where the level of natural abundance is such that any diminution in material comfort which would be occasioned by their implementation could likely be accommodated. That nation is Canada.

This cursory discussion barely scratches the surface of Blake's genius. However, my objective is modest: to point out that the divine is situated within the human consciousness and that if it is incorporated explicitly into our decision processes, the possibility of transcendence is enhanced. By way of summary, it can be indicated that this idea has at least two practical applications.

First, the suggestion that divinely inspired transcendence should be the objective of action implies that human accomplishments should be evaluated by a criterion which originates outside the *idea of progress*. Only this approach offers the possibility of deliverance from an inferior life-trajectory. Second, transcendence involves the codetermination of action by contraries such as reason and the imagination. Further, these two elements must be held in a particular relationship to each other: they become intrinsic in the sense that one cannot be defined without reference to the other; nevertheless, they remain as opposites because they obey different imperatives; they are dynamic and the dimensions of their interpenetration is subject to continual change over time; they command equal status. This relationship, which can be generalized to encompass other phenomena, is different from that which exists between discrete opposites such as rationalism and romanticism. Together, reason and imagination can form a totality – an optimally configured conscious-ness – and when combined with nature, they form another totality: reality. In a later chapter, these types of intrinsic, dynamic, linked relationships will be discussed in more detail, and conditions in which they occur will be defined as a *tense dialectic*, in which the latter word can be interpreted as follows:

Two concepts are dialectically related when the elaboration of one draws attention to the other as an opposed concept; when … the opposite concept is required for the validity … of the first; and when one finds that the real theoretical problem is that of [determining] the interrelationship between the two concepts. (Diesing 1971, 212)

This idea is important, for if the creation of tense dialectics is a precondition of transcendence and transcendence is an element of universal knowledge, the methodology and ideas included in a gestalt economics discipline should be patterned accordingly. I will return to consider these economic implications in due course; first, it is necessary to elaborate more fully upon the meaning of universal knowledge.

Blake's theme has persisted over time as an important component of the underground of knowledge that exists outside the *idea of progress*. It has been criticized, interpreted, modified, and extended in numerous ways. One of the most useful extensions was devised by Søren Kierkegaard. He too was a global thinker, but I wish to examine only a small subset of his theory. In particular, I wish to show how he reinforced the idea that there is transcendence beyond the rational and the imaginative, and how he related this concept to the immanent divinity of man.

Before discussing these contributions, it is necessary to make some general comments. Neither Blake nor Kierkegaard are easy to under-stand. Blake's imagery is obscure and Kierkegaard is elusive because he often adopts a provocative, Socratic stance to initiate debate. Fur-thermore, they are difficult to compare because they employ different genres and are responding to different cultural circumstances. Nev-ertheless, they are soul mates because they share an antipathy towards the *idea of progress* and seek means by which mankind can achieve a more fulfilling existence. About this issue, Kierkegaard is not obscure, for among his more vivid invectives are included "modernity is humbug" and "all corruption comes ultimately from the natural sciences."

Ironically, Kierkegaard lays the groundwork for his theory of the divine-seeking imagination in a book that does not mention it, *Either/Or*. This is a fable in which a romantic and a rationalist criticize each others' world-views. The romantic points out some of the deficiencies of rational existence, condemning the tendency to construct unrealistic paradigms and to pursue mundane objectives with statements such as:

What the philosophers [economists?] say about Reality is often as disappointing as the sign you see in the shop window, which reads: Pressing Done Here. If you brought your clothes to be pressed, you would be fooled; for only the sign is for sale. (Kierkegaard 1959, 31)

and:

Of all ridiculous things, it seems to me the most ridiculous is to be a busy man of affairs, prompt to meals, and prompt to work. Hence when I see a fly settle down in a crucial moment on the nose of a business man, or see him bespattered by a carriage which passes by him in even greater haste, or a drawbridge opens before him, or a tile from the roof falls down and strikes him dead, then I laugh heartily. And who could help laughing? What do they accomplish, these hustlers? Are they not like the housewife, when her house was on fire, who in her excitement saved the fire-tongs? What more do they save from the great fire of life? (Kierkegaard 1959, 24)

In short, the rational life is unfulfilling. By leading a life according to externally imposed rules of conduct, man represses aspects of his character so that every act is accompanied by a lingering sense of regret emanating from that which is repressed. However, the romantic life is also inferior because, though emotive attributes are exercised freely, it is profligate and egotistical. One is invariably confronted with the realization that there is a widening disparity between actual and potential.

The leitmotif of *Either/Or* is that an unspiritual life – be it romantic or rational – is laden with regret and anxiety, which can only be overcome by elevating man's consciousness to include the divine-seeking imagination. To do so, man must have faith that there is deliverance and that he is discerning enough to make the choices which foster rather than impede that deliverance. The twist (a K-twist?) is that it takes courage to enter this new and unknown realm because it does not have any rational antecedents, for "faith begins precisely where thinking leaves off." It is a realm where one is surrounded by the unknown and must make decisions without reference to external rules or without knowledge of their consequences; where there is heightened awareness of the limitations of human understanding relative to the mysteries of the cosmos; where there are misgivings about the strength of one's commitment if faced with adversity. Under such circumstances one is likely to be hesitant and fearful or, in Kierkegaard's terms, experience *dread*. This is the essence of his theory: that to nurture a divine-seeking imagination, one must have faith but also be cognizant that it will be accompanied by dread and that the two concepts must be held together in a tense dialectic relationship. The irony is that to avoid the anxieties of rationalism one must adopt a stance in which a heightened form of anxiety, dread, is sustained. To quote him, "Everything turns on dread coming into view ... dread is the first reflex of possibility, a shimmer yet a fearful enchantment" (Kierkegaard 1957, 39; 1967, 41), Faith and dread coexist as preconditions to the discovery of truth, which Kierkegaard defines as follows: "An objective uncertainty held fast in an approximation process of the most passionate inwardness is the truth, the highest truth attainable for an existing individual" (Kierkegaard 1946, 214). For one schooled within the *idea of progress*, it is difficult to accept the concept that truth has nothing to do with certainty. Rather, it is the dynamic process by which the individual with a passionate commitment to the divine-seeking imagination probes the unknown. Unfortunately, because this probe cannot be undertaken without experiencing dread, most of us find some excuse to avoid the journey.

This particular thread of Kierkegaard's thinking is helpful to us for several reasons. First, it identifies a tense dialectic within the imagination itself that helps to explain why the relationship between reason and imagination is so often dominated by the former (i.e., the imagination is engaged in an internal struggle). Second, it indicates that either anxiety or dread is an immanent aspect of the human condition and that of the two, dread is the more fearful but must nevertheless be embraced if truth is to be discovered. At the practical level, this position infers that policies designed to eliminate or suppress anxiety – of which there are many – are misguided unless they involve a transcendence toward dread. Struggle is not something to be avoided in the interest of material comfort; it is something to be redirected from the mundane to more noble pursuits. Third, we have a new definition of truth that is dramatically different from the way the concept is perceived in orthodox economics. It will need to be considered in any reformulation of the discipline.

Kierkegaard's ideas have become the focus of many diverse intellectual inquiries. For example, his belief that dread is part of the human condition and should be confronted rather than repressed is a central tenet of the school of existential philosophy he helped to originate, and his related insight that "irony is like the negative way, not the truth, but the way to the truth" has undoubtedly given confidence to many post-modern humanists employing an ironic mode of expression. (See Pynchon 1973.) However, my own objective is to take what is admittedly an elusive concept and ground it in reality so that it will be useful for explaining everyday economic processes. Fortunately, Paul Tillich has formalized the Kierkegaard scheme in such a way that this purpose can be accomplished. (See Tillich 1951 and Martin 1971.) His starting point is Kierkegaard's observation that "man is a synthesis of the infinite and the finite, of the temporal and the eternal, of freedom and necessity." Tillich's theory is described in the next section.

A SYSTEMATIC FRAMEWORK

Tillich is recognized as one of the most formidable Protestant thinkers of the century. One of his contributions was to formalize an ontological theory that systematizes Christian existentialism and does not do violence to the broader aspects of either Blake or Kierkegaard. Before describing his schema, two preliminary comments are warranted. First, the three scholars in question employ similar categories but use different terminology. In order to minimize confusion, Tillich's definitions are reinterpreted to correspond to the terms that have already been used, reserving as bracketed, italicized addenda those terms he actually used. Second, we are obviously into the realm of gestalt theory where verification is not possible. Tillich was aware of this fact but felt that the deficiency is far less telling than the fragmentation and misrepresentation of reality which accompanies analysis undertaken within the confines of pure reason. A paraphrase of his position provides a summary statement of the whole thrust of the search for universal knowledge.

Knowledge stands in a dilemma; experimental knowledge is safe but may not ultimately be significant, while ontological knowledge can be ultimately significant but cannot be proven. I prefer significance to verifiability.

Tillich begins by defining ontological reason. It comprises the totality of individual consciousness and includes four interacting components similar to Blake's four Zoas. The first is technical reason, which refers to egocentrically oriented cognitive processes undertaken to verify empirical propositions or to construct logical analysis; it is the attribute, indeed the only attribute, possessed by *economic man*. The other three components are products of the imagination (*aesthetic, organizational,* and *organic reason*) and relate to the pursuit

Figure 2
Tillich's Ontological Framework

1. Components of Ontological Existence	
Technical Reason	Imagination (comprised of aesthetic, organizational, and organic reason)

2. Poles and Dimesions of the Ontological Structure that Constrains
   Human Choices

Selfhood	Eternal/Infinity
Individualization	Participation
Dynamics	Form
Freedom	Destiny

of beauty, justice, and love, attributes of divinity. Meaningful existence requires the simultaneous existence and energetic pursuit of all four components. One must not dominate the others: if technical reason dominates, the system collapses into an *idea of progress* mentality; if technical reason is dominated, we have a chaotic life of ungrounded anarchy. Here we have the distinction between rationality, imagination, and transcendence that resembles the theories of Blake and Kierkegaard.

It is next postulated that, given his ontological reason, man is capable of understanding relational truth and the fact that the choice mechanism which guides his actions is embedded in a four-dimensional ontological structure in which each dimension is bounded by bi-polar opposites: finite selfhood and eternal infinity, individualization and participation, dynamics and form, and freedom and destiny. For reference purposes, these dimensions are identified in Figure 2. The selfhood-eternal/infinity continuum is the basis of the subject-object structure of reason and recognizes the spatial and temporal limits of man relative to the infinite and eternal universe. The other three dimensions are simply more specific manifestations of this dichotomy. Individualization allows the self to exercise its own unique attributes in the development of a persona, while participation involves the suppression of individuality to serve the larger human community. Dynamics involves intentionality and vitality, while form refers to acceptable forms of behaviour that constrain that vitality. Freedom refers to the processes of reflection and decision, as well as the responsibility for the consequences that flow from these decisions. It is constrained by one's sense of destiny, about which Tillich states, "It includes the communities to which I belong, the past unremembered and remembered, the environment which has shaped me. It refers to all my former decisions. Destiny is not a strange power which determines what shall happen to me. It is myself as given, formed by nature, history and myself" (Tillich 1951, 185).

There are several things to note about this system. First, it can be observed that the structure is comprised of four egocentric poles and four outer-world poles. The outer-world poles involve the unknown, and it is here that Tillich intersects with Kierkegaard. One must have faith to believe that these outer-world forces are not pernicious but rather provide man with the opportunity to achieve deliverance, even though such faith is accompanied by dread. That is, the Blake-Kierkegaard imagination extends man from indulgence in the self by expanding his ontological structure.

Second, in each dimension the poles are related intrinsically: "Without individualization nothing would exist to be related. Without participation the category or relation would have no basis in reality … my destiny is the basis of my freedom; my freedom participates in the shaping of my destiny" (Tillich 1951, 177, 185). However, the relationship should not be haphazard, but rather one involving tension. It is Tillich's primary thesis *that meaningful existence requires that tension be preserved between each bi-polar pair* or, as the idea was referred to earlier, that it be a tense dialectic relationship. If they become unhinged, chaos or ennui ensue; if one pole dominates the other, the consequence is either excessive egotism or ungrounded uncertainty. Neither condition is conducive to meaningful existence and discovery of the truth. Each pole must be an effective counterforce to prevent abuses arising from the excesses of its opposite. The fear that they will cease to interact is referred to as the "anxiety of existential disruption."

Third, recall that meaningful existence also requires that there be tension between reason and the imagination. In this, Tillich echoes Blake and Kierkegaard, and his only substantive contribution is to suggest that the three main elements of the divine-seeking imagination involve the pursuit of beauty, justice, and truth. I shall discuss the idea of justice at a later stage and for now only wish to draw attention to where it is situated in Tillich's theoretical system.

This, then, is Tillich's ontological framework. Each of four elements of ontological existence (*technical, aesthetic, organization,* and *organic reason*) has associated with it four bi-polar dimensions uniting opposites. Meaningful existence requires that the relationship between the elements in ontological reason and the opposites in the ontological structure be tense and dialectic. He then employs this framework to analyse human actuality using the anxiety of existential disruption as his point of departure.

To Tillich, the irony of Western existence is that faced with this anxiety, the typical response is counter-productive. When threatened by forces we cannot control and understand as represented by the outer-world poles, we respond by shrinking our attention to egocentric issues, thereby eliminating the tension that is necessary for a meaningful existence. This self-elevation is the irony: in a misguided attempt to protect ourselves from external uncertainties, we behave in a way that deprives life of its potential for transcendence. That is, in order to eliminate his exposure to chance, man also eliminates the possibility of excellence. (See Strauss 1959.)

Self-elevation has become the central feature of Western man's existence. It is reflected in three related attitudes that Tillich refers to as unbelief, hubris, and concupiscence. Unbelief is the abandonment of faith and is reflected in a variety of secular behavioural patterns, such as a reliance on ratiocination, a denial of mystery, and a preference for contract justice in which fairness is defined in terms of man-made laws. Hubris is arrogance and is expressed intellectually in the substitution of the understandable partial truth for the unknown ultimate truth, morally in the substitution of situational ethics for universal ethics, and in economic policy in the assertion that unforeseen disruptions of fragile eco-systems can be rectified by technological ingenuity. Concupiscence, narrowly defined as lust, also has a wider connotation and includes all aspects of man's striving to satisfy physical wants and the thirst for power and wealth.

It can be observed that unbelief, hubris, and concupiscence translate rather easily into rational, striving self-interest, the characteristics of *economic man*. Viewed in this light, a discipline such as orthodox economics, which includes this conceptualization within its axiomatic structure, is not a progressive science but rather is seen to be contributing to a state of affairs that is contrary to meaningful existence. Given this, the need for disciplinary reform seems to become more urgent.

However, there are also positive ways in which Tillich's theory can help to better our understanding of economic processes and eventually to contribute to the design of an alternative disciplinary paradigm to reflect these processes. For example, the impacts of the preference-shaping technologies that have become the deterministic vehicles for actualizing the *idea of progress* can be evaluated with reference to Tillich's ontological theory. Three relevant impacts are discernible. First, they have eroded the aesthetic, organizational, and organic components of ontological reason, leaving the technical component to dominate. Second, they have eroded the outer-world poles so that they have been dominated by the egocentric poles. Third, the dynamics of technological change provides a vitality that is a substitute for ontological tension and creates the illusion that the latter is not required for meaningful existence. These effects warrant a brief description.

An analysis of the extent to which technical reason dominates other modes of thought in industrial society was already presented in chapter two. However, it can now be augmented by supporting observations that are more appropriate to the terminology of the present discussion. For example, Ellul has stated, "There is no room in practical activity for gratuitous aesthetic occupation ... the rules obeyed in a technical organization are no longer rules of justice or injustice ... technique must reduce man to a technical animal, the king of the slaves of technique. Human caprice crumbles before this necessity; there can be no human autonomy in the face of technical autonomy ... progress consists of progressive dehumanization" (Ellul 1964, 73, 133, 138, viii). Weber also developed this last idea in great detail. In fact, the most persistent theme in all his work is the observation that, while the stated objective of technological expansion invariably relates to the control of nature, its real consequence is that morality and justice are "imprisoned within an iron cage" of technical reason. (See Smart 1983, 125.) In other words, technology co-opts the imagination.

Technology also contributes to the erosion of the four outer-world poles. The unknowable is ignored and action is based on the presumption that everything significant is knowable provided that one is sufficiently committed to research; the eternal is neglected as technology makes man increasingly myopic; participation is thwarted because populations are fragmented into internally homogeneous, but isolated, interest groups, each defined with reference to a specialized subset of the knowledge required to operate the technological apparatus; form is weakened as man gains more and more confidence about physical, biological, and social engineering; the marvels of innovation create the impression that man's destiny is his freedom. Orthodox economics has a role in all these deceptions. For example, it has contributed to myopia by fostering a set of evaluation techniques that overlook the long-run consequences of industrialization. On the production side there are a variety of conventions that shorten time horizons: nature's bounty is viewed as free, so that the supply price of natural resources only reflects extraction costs; real discount rates are high; producers are not expected to pay for the social costs of waste disposal; oligopolistic pricing permits premature obsolescence. On the consumption side, preference-shifting technologies that advocate immediate gratification and conspicuous consumption are condoned as long as they operate through the market place. In short, technology and its superstructure reduce the significance of both the unknowable and the eternal in man's consciousness.

Finally, technology imposes its own dynamic, which creates the illusion that ontological tension is unnecessary. This dynamic involves the moulding of a conforming population that periodically has its consumption behaviour energized by the introduction of a new style. In both the moulding and the energizing, the preference-shaping electronic media plays a central role. Huge masses of supposedly independent individuals are mobilized into a homogeneous audience who share the common comfort of identifying with the superstars of culture, athletics, and politics and who simultaneously become a mass market in which prevailing designs and styles become universal standards and symbols of cohesion; thus opiated, this market is periodically aroused by the introduction of new designs and stimulated by the idea that novelty equates with progress. The vitality and exhilaration of change seems to make ontological tension redundant. This idea is explored by scholars such as Cox (1966) and Scitovsky (1976) and summarized succinctly by Eliot's (1964) well-known observation that in spite of endless invention and experiment we have "knowledge of words, but ignorance of the Word."

Thus, Tillich's theory provides a framework for describing the human potential, as well as an explanation of how the human psyche has been shrunk by the *idea of progress*. In the following chapters it will be assumed that the potential he describes is a reasonable representation of universal knowledge. If we revert to the terminology of the three scholars who have been examined, it can be said that in Blake's terms it involves the elevation of the divine-seeking imagination to facilitate transcendence, to Kierkegaard it is attainment of faith and the commitment to search for truth in spite of dread, and to Tillich it is the expansion of ontological reason while retaining tension between the egocentric and outer-world poles of one's ontological structure. In spite of the diversity in terminology, there is sufficient correspondence to justify treating them as a single conceptualization of meaningful existence.

4 Local Knowledge

Schizophrenia may be
our greatest source of strength.

Our task now is to identify Canadian local knowledge, the normative principles that should guide the national conscience. To be authentic, it must embody the interpenetrations between our history and those contemporary physical and human environments that distinguish us from other national groups. On the surface, it might seem that such a task is futile because the Canadian reality is so diverse. We are a mosaic with at least two solitudes, a heartland linked with parochial hinterlands; we are elusive and unpredictable because we are vulnerable to the vicissitudes of nature and international events; we have difficulty defining our identity, perhaps because of our protean history or perhaps because, as one poet has observed, it is difficult to discover your cadence in colonized space. Under such circumstances, distinctive regularities are not easy to identify.

However, it is possible that the search for surface regularities is misguided, for often they are the result of an orderliness imposed to constrain more fundamental underlying forces. In fact, given the views about technology discussed in the previous chapter, this is very likely to be the case in a nation such as Canada, dedicated to the *idea of progress*. Thus, it may be more fruitful to search for our local knowledge among the forces that make the imposition of regularities and order necessary.

This is the domain of humanists, so we must turn to them for inspiration. The task is slippery, with at least two formidable pitfalls: how does one determine which humanists are best able to articulate the particularities of Canadian existence and how can one be sure that their ideas are being interpreted accurately? Neither question can be answered definitively; analysis can only be judged *ex post facto* in terms of plausibility and reasonableness. The following discussion should be evaluated accordingly.

I believe that the essence of Canadian local knowledge is captured in the work of Margaret Atwood, Harold Innis, and Alex Colville. Further, I believe that it can be shown that they share a common theme, which, when translated into the ponderous language of the social scientist, is:

In order to maintain the integrity of the nation, tension must be maintained between a set of fundamental bi-polar opposites which characterize Canadian existence.

At the outset, two definitional problems need to be addressed. First, the word "integrity" carries the dual meaning of worthiness and wholeness. Second, "fundamental" implies a particular subset of all the oppositional forces. While these elements will be identified as the discussion proceeds, in general terms the word refers to those in which a case can be made to support the sanctity of each pole. For example, efficiency and equality are fundamental opposites; good and evil are not.

While the discussion will be confined to the work of the three humanists mentioned above, it should be noted that this theme is not uncommon. For example, similar ideas are articulated by Mac-Lennan (1945), Grant (1969), Lee (1977), and Woodcock (1989). A reviewer of this last book has said the following, "Woodcock finds deep political, regional, ethnic and class tensions: French confronted English, radicals did battle with tories, women fought for equality, newcomers struggled against an intolerant and often racist majority, and all Canadians had to grapple with a northern environment that seemed to frustrate every attempt to build a country. These tensions, however, did not destroy Canada. On the contrary, they helped to create a different type of nation" (Westfall 1989, C7). These observations relate to the nineteenth century. Hence, it seems that there are historical data available to support the validity of the proposition that is being advanced.

MARGARET ATWOOD

Atwood is an eminent Canadian poet-novelist with wide ranging interests. For example, "she has been called a feminist writer, for her incisive commentaries on sex roles; a religious writer, for her visions of spiritual ecstasy; a gothic writer, for her images of grotesques, misfits and surreal disorientations of the psyche; a writer of the Canadian wilderness; a nationalist writer; a regionalist" (Rosenberg 1984, 15). In spite of this eclecticism, there is some consensus that her poetry has a dominant thread, constructed from the entwining of a number of identifiable strands. My reading leads me to believe that there are six such strands which are particularly significant. First, the universe is conceptualized as a set of related binary opposites, among the more important of which are male-female, civilization-nature, and spatial-temporal. Second, integrity requires that tension be preserved between these opposites. Third, if tension dissipates, the relationship degenerates into either isolation or domination. Fourth, in the male-female dimension, male domination is actualized through technology and mythology. Fifth, each pole in the system has a dual connectedness. That is, a pole (e.g., female) is connected to its opposite (male) and also to complementary poles in other dimensions (e.g., nature and time). This concept implies, for example, that women have particular responsibilities as stewards of nature and, relatedly, for maintaining temporal sensitivities. Sixth, the conceptual arrangement has metaphorical potential so that individual and community dimensions can be linked. For example, the United States can be perceived as a dominant male.

This is not an exhaustive list, and of course not every strand is present in every poem. Nevertheless, it is instructive to examine some of her work in order to illustrate these propositions and also to demonstrate that there are parallels between her paradigm and that which was being posited as a framework for universal knowledge.

Most of the strands identified above are visible in *The Journals of Susanna Moodie*. These poems are fictionalized accounts of the experiences of a real nineteenth-century Canadian pioneer as she seeks to ascribe meaning to her immigrant venture into the wilderness and subsequent relocation to a more structured, artificial urban environment. Throughout, Mrs Moodie is encompassed in dilemmas between "violent dualities": divided sensibilities that tear at her conscience and also elude her comprehension. Initially, she feels alienated as a settler in an unresponsive land, a "word in a foreign language," but persists only to discover that when she wants to "love this country," she becomes appalled at nature's destructiveness; when young, she cannot give herself over to the wilds and "let the animals inhabit her," yet on ageing, she becomes sufficiently penetrated by its spirit to "be no longer fit for the world" of manners and progress; nevertheless she must leave the wilderness and face the new anxieties of urban technology, madness, and the prospect of death sitting "every day ... on a stuffed sofa" and listening to the "shrill of glass and steel."

Critical response to the *Journals* is overwhelmingly positive, and it is agreed that the essence of Canada's historical struggle is skilfully represented by Mrs Moodie's transformations. She begins as an alienated pioneer, experiences periods of reluctant, painful, and fearful, acceptance of the wilderness culminating in an attitude of passionate reverence for nature, only to be uprooted and relocated amidst distasteful urban technology. The poems also provide an insight into Atwood's vision for the future. The genius of that vision is the recognition that Mrs Moodie's wisdom stems from her unwillingness to succumb to the temptation to make a total commitment to either the self or the unknown, to either nature or civilization, to either hope or despair. She internalizes the tensions between these opposing forces, seeing that personal fortitude needs to be juxtaposed against the unknown, that the terror and chaotic order of nature need to penetrate the comfort and visible orderliness of technological civilization, and that tragedy is ameriorated by hope as, for example, when she sadly buries her dead son but plants him in this country "like a flag."

At the conceptual level, the *Journals* also provide a remarkable insight into the array of forces that make it difficult to sustain these tensions. The human mind is shown to be reluctant to deliberately internalize oppositions because of the ambiguity and discord inherent in the process. That is, it requires courage and stamina to willfully substitute complexity for simplicity. Furthermore, the poles that anchor the tensions are themselves fickle and dynamic. A particularly vivid example is presented in a poem titled "The Two Fires." In a summer wilderness fire, the trees melt and Mrs Moodie is cut off from escape to a nearby lake. She is saved by staying in her house and concentrating on the "logic of windows," the straight lines and shapes that dispute chaos. In a winter fire, the house shrivels in the flames and becomes a threat. Now it is the snow-laden open air that protects her. She concludes that "each refuge fails / us; each danger becomes a haven." However, the experiences leave her with new insights for they "left charred marks / now around which I / try to grow." (See Rosenberg 1984, 44.) Grace (1980) presents other examples from Atwood's work in which the struggle with dynamic opposites becomes the focus of human endeavour.

The third and fourth strands are perhaps best illustrated in Atwood's feminist poetry, where an overriding theme is that if tension is allowed to dissipate, personal evolution is deflected onto an inferior trajectory characterized by either isolation or domination. The destructiveness of both afflictions is examined.

Often, lovers share physical space but are emotionally distant and isolated, as for example when "your mouth is nothingness / when it touches me I vanish" (Atwood 1972a, 53). Neither partner can grow and their personas wither and atrophy. However, isolation extends far beyond gender relationships. The observation "This is not a debate / but a duet / with two deaf singers" (Atwood 1978, 75) is a universal, applicable to a range of situations we have all experienced and observed.

An even more persistent theme is domination, particularly in sexual relationships. Using wit and vivid imagery, Atwood explores the strategies and intentions of male imperialism. Women are subjected to pain rather than ecstacy when "you fit into me / like a hook into an eye / a fish hook / an open eye" and are stroked by male hands to become "like the moon / seen from the earth," realizing that word plays are political devices designed to transform a partner into a subject and concluding, "You are the sun / in reverse, all energy / flows into you and is / abolished; ... I lie mutilated beside you" (Atwood 1972a, 1; 1978, 11; 1972a, 47). Throughout her work, Atwood exposes the raw edges of subjugation. One commentator concludes that identifying with this circumstance as a woman "requires recognizing oneself as a being whose flesh is colonized, whose eyes are captured behind mirrors, whose words are helpless" (Blakely 1983, 47).

Male domination is buttressed by both mythology and technology. In the mythical realm, societies and households have been patriarchal since classical times, and Atwood portrays the consequences of giving primacy to the sun-father over the earth-mother, the sun over the moon, Apollo over Artemis, and Adam over Eve. Further, she demonstrates that contemporary culture "mimics the classical in its portrayal of male heroes and female handmaidens" (see Davey 1984, 21) and argues passionately that deliverance must supersede conquest.

In the technological realm, male rationalism shapes the world according to the dictates of the *idea of progress*. Canadian males have a particularly fertile field for such initiatives because of the abundance of resources and wildernesses and have responded by creating an elaborate artificial world of tools and toys: ploughs and power mowers, highways and hockey sticks, superstructures and service clubs.

The basic logic of technology seems benign enough: nature can be destructive and niggardly, so man must design an alternative reality

that is more secure and generous. But to Atwood the more fundamental consequence of technology is to reinforce male primacy by
developing instruments and techniques that entrench existing patterns of privilege and by desecrating the domains over which woman
has custody. Interestingly, the camera is identified as a symbol of
desecration in the temporal domain. Because it creates a "still-life," it
is able to abstract from time and thereby to eliminate a sphere of
female sensibilities. But the still-life picture has an even more pernicious effect because within it the relationship between cause and
effect is blurred. When elements are juxtaposed in space rather than
related sequentially, they are susceptible to arbitrary interpretations.
Consequently, they are likely to be defined from inside the dominant
paradigm rather than with reference to the real and the true. Life's
immanent rhythms, the territory of the female, are ignored as the
world is interpreted in terms of rational, spatial, male-oriented
concepts.

   An example connecting the second and fifth strands, and one that
is particularly relevant to Canadian experience and the *idea of progress*,
is described in "The Progressive Insanities of the Pioneer." Here, a
male pioneer, already partly crazed because he has allowed rationality
to fracture his own psyche, tries to impose civilizing order on his
property by creating a house, fences, and furrows. He does so
because unstructured space causes him anxiety. "He asserted / into
the furrows, I / am not random." But nature has resilience and is not
easily conquered. The pioneer's attempt to dominate fails, at first
gently "The ground / replied with aphorisms: / a tree-sprout, a
nameless / weed, words / he couldn't understand" (Atwood 1968, 36)
– but then more persistently, and in the end he is destroyed by the
"unnamed whale" of natural process as it bursts through his fences
and his subject-object categorizing mind.

   Interspersed throughout Atwood's other work are similar warnings
that attempts to dominate the processes of nature are inevitably self-
destructive. If man appears to succeed in his conquest, the emotive
elements of his psyche that are required for wisdom and fulfilment
wither; if he fails, the knowledge of his insignificance leads to anxiety.
Man thus imprisons himself within technology and resembles the
animals in "Dreams of the Animals," who, once caged, can no longer
discover the patterns of existence that preserve their species but
instead must dream of escape and wake to a madness in which they
run "all day in figure eights."

   The transfer of Atwood's themes about technological domination
from personal relationships to the national consciousness, our sixth
strand, is an easy step. The United States is the continental male, the

technological dynamo, intent on conquering whatever it can see within an "ever-receding horizon." Canada is a target in this spread of hegemony, and our natural endowments are pillaged accordingly. Atwood alerts us that we must see America as it really is – "as you move, the air in front of you / blossoms with targets" (Atwood 1968, 50) – and for our own sakes, as well as theirs, *resist*.

My window is a funnel
for the shapes of chaos
In the backyard, frozen bones, the childrens'
voices, derelict
objects

Inside, the wall
buckles; the pressure

balanced by this clear
small silence.

We must resist. We must refuse
to disappear
                    Atwood 1968, 29

Atwood explores the viability of various resistance strategies, suggesting that in some ways the female and national plights are analogous. In her feminist pieces, women are shown to have options: if they wish solely to preserve their sanity within a patriarchal system, they may be either stoic or escapist; if they wish to modify the system, they must seek to transcend their oppression. It is the latter stance that is of most relevance but to put it in sharper relief, the alternatives can be described briefly.

To be stoic is to succumb, at least outwardly, to male dominance and, like old Mrs Moodie, to wait patiently for the time when it will be displaced by some force from "outside the circle." Just as the dinosaurs were defeated by their own limited knowledge, pushed out "by the velvet immoral / uncalloused and armourless mammals" so too will technological man be defeated by his own tunnel vision. To be escapist is to transfer one's energy to alternative realms, thereby deflecting the frustration of being oppressed. That is, one can reject male aggressiveness and seek to construct a personal space which has a more satisfying feminist perspective. Women who have escaped, while "living within the male architecture of walls, tables, cleanliness and glass" have loyalties in "another realm of decay, growth and organic change."

Both stoicism and escapism involve disengagement and a weakened stewardship role. The more challenging alternative is to transcend the male world of "rationalized time and articulated space" and create one "of pre-articulate process," which is strong enough to retain its integrity when set against the reality of the *idea of progress*. It has been argued that the central objective of Atwood's early novels is to describe the contours of this creative transition and that "the structural similarities between the books are impressive – alienation from natural process, followed by descent into a more primitive but healing reality, and finally some return to personal wholeness through renewed recognition of natural forces" (Davey 1984, 59). Two points are worth noting. First, the catharsis involves a restoration to a state of organic growth rather than rational order and, as such, is a mechanism for transforming the *idea of progress* mentality. Second, the pattern of transcendence is identical to the myth of deliverance. It thus presents a program of restoration that, in form at least, is consistent with universal knowledge.

If applied to national issues, Atwoodian transcendence involves the search for a new angle of vision to perceive the Canadian reality which breaks the enclosing circle of male rationality and takes courage from the fact that "All peoples are driven / to the point of eating their gods / after a time" (Atwood 1984, 13). The elevation of subjugated values implied by this process is exemplified by Susanna Moodie, who continually transposes dominating relationships into tense opposites. However, the idea is also captured in "Progressive Insanities," which suggests that the pioneer could have survived had he let the threatening wilderness inside his space rather than try to exclude it. "If he had known unstructured / space is a deluge / and stocked his log house- / boat with all the animals / even the wolves, / he might have floated" (Atwood 1968, 38). This conceptualization raises an important point about the attitude implicit in this new perception. Those of us who have been conditioned by the *idea of progress* have become addicted to more than materialism and rationalism. We have become accustomed to *order* because the simplification and fragmentation that it embodies seem to be necessary if one is to make sense out of a complex reality. What is being proposed is a different intellectual stance. Survival requires that one realize that the ambiguities, conflicts, incoherences, and ironies of the Canadian existence need to be incorporated into our field of vision rather than suppressed, and once inside need to be nurtured until a new,

transcendent level of comprehension is attained. What the imagination is to Blake and dread is to Kierkegaard, dissonance seems to be
to Atwood because one could capture the essence of her stance by
modifying Kierkegaard's statements "Everything turns on dissonance
coming into view ... dissonance is the first reflex of possibility, a
shimmer yet a fearful enchantment." (See page 51.) Furthermore, as
one critic has observed, she is telling us that we must view dissonance as an ironic, schizophrenic gift. "It is typical of Atwood,
however, to portray our national schizophrenia not simply as illness
or weakness, but as our greatest potential strength" (Grace 1980, 33).

Atwood is echoing a view held by other insightful humanists. For
example, her stance resembles Hegel's quest for spirit, Havel's plea
for a refocused political agenda, environmentalists' reverence for
native cosmology (see Guédon 1983), and even the yin-yang structure
of Eastern religion. It is also a common theme amongst novelists.
Mann describes a musical masterpiece as follows: "The whole work
is dominated by the paradox (if it is a paradox) that in it dissonance
stands for the expression of everything lofty, solemn, pious, everything of the spirit; while consonance and firm tonality are reserved
for the world of hell, in this context a world of banality and commonplace" (Mann 1986, 361). Bellow has Herzog observe that his
estranged wife's mental disorder is "super clarity." Rushie comments
that "incoherence will have its day." The concept has also been the
subject of more theoretical analysis. (See Laing 1959 and Deleuse
and Guattari 1983.) Atwood is simply arguing that a distinctive Canadian model be formulated around this elemental idea.

From the foregoing it is apparent that Atwood's nationalism
involves more than an attempt to carve out an avaricious Canadian
niche in the reality of global materialism. She argues that Canada's
geographic, political, and economic position on the edge of empire
gives us a unique angle of vision from which to view the world
industrial order, and we have the social responsibility to articulate a
thoughtful, humane view in the interest of species survival, and not
merely for national interest.

In summary, if this interpretation of Atwood is reasonable, we
have a coherent framework to use as a basis for local knowledge. It
has several positive features, not the least of which is its compatibility
with our conceptualization of universal knowledge. (For example,
there is a correspondence between Atwood's treatment of domination
and isolation and Tillich's notion of the anxiety of existential disruption.) In addition, the fact that her model includes interdimensional
linkages means that there is, potentially at least, an opportunity to

extend it and to construct an even more comprehensive gestalt model suitable for the analysis of other local realms, including economic processes. In order to assess the plausibility of such extensions, it is useful to examine the ideas of the man who is probably recognized as Canada's most distinguished political economist.

HAROLD INNIS

Innis was dedicated to the belief that Canadian social scientists should ground their studies in the realities of the nation's technologies, institutions, and geography. A sceptical observer might note that his writing is dated and historically oriented and therefore be tempted to conclude that his work is not relevant to a contemporary society dominated by technologies he never experienced: television, computers, high-speed transportation, electronic data networks. Ironically, the truth is just the opposite. Innis developed an understanding of the principles that underlie economic forces in Canada, and his appeal is actually enhanced by the flow of subsequent events because his theories have withstood the test of time and thus are not only relevant but authenticated.

Innis's two most notable theoretical accomplishments are in the realms of staple resources and communications. Together, they provide an insightful explanation of many of the forces that have shaped Canada's development pattern. In describing his contribution it is not my intent to be comprehensive; rather, it is simply to examine the structure of his paradigm with reference to our own hypothesized framework and, if they are compatible, to see how they might be combined.

At the outset, a semantic problem needs to be addressed. It arises because Innis was a man of moderation who typically spoke of "balance between opposing forces so as to avoid bias." It seems reasonable to translate this concept to mean "tension between opposites so as to avoid domination." That is to say, unbiased balance between opposing forces is achieved by creating a new force out of their interpenetration that encapsulates the tension between them. Indeed, critics and reviewers of Innis's work continually refer to the acuity with which he incorporates opposing forces into his conceptual framework. To illustrate this characteristic, consider the following statements by different commentators.

He focused on conflicting forces and on action/reaction sequences as part of his own form of dialectic analysis.

He found the paradigm [he sought] by focusing upon the tensions that defined the problem itself – the tension between the metropolis and the hinterland, the tension between what was inside and what was outside.

Innis' most remarkable and original insight is that the tension between media of time and media of space is a reflex of the centre/margin thesis in Canadian economic history.

His hatred of oppressive social institutions led him to examine the manner of their subversion from many angles.

These statements suggest that the moderation of Innis's written work reflected his humility rather than the intensity of his concern. Nevertheless, the validity of the following interpretation of his work hinges somewhat on the reasonableness of making the semantic leap from "balance without bias" to "tension without domination."

It is convenient to begin the discussion with an outline of the staples thesis and its implications. These can be summarized as follows:

- Canadian staples are financed primarily by foreign capital and are developed to serve international markets.
- The distribution of Canadian resources is uneven, and hence there is regional concentration of staples industries. Because of the timing of discoveries and the nature of foreign demand, the staples have been developed serially (i.e., fur, fish, timber, minerals, wheat, and in the post-Innis era, oil and gas, and hydroelectricity).
- Development of depleting staple resources tends to follow a long cycle in which there is an initial spurt of capital formation followed by a long period of extraction and rent generation until exhaustion. Superimposed on the extraction phase is a layer of resource-augmenting investment. Normally, inventories are such that the resource owner has considerable flexibility as to when this augmentation will occur. Hence he has leverage over any government that is seeking to influence the timing of his investment in order to contribute to its own macroeconomic objectives.
- Within this long cycle there are instabilities caused by the vicissitudes of international commodities markets and variations in supply conditions.
- Most staple industries have both monopolistic and monopsonistic characteristics. The former arise because of barriers to entry associated with scale economies, capital requirements, vertical and horizontal integration, and so on. Monopsonistic elements normally

arise where large firms are situated in specialized regions and are thus able to dominate the communities in which they operate.
• The externalities of staple development imprint the region and nation with both infrastructure and superstructure networks.

When these characteristics are seen *in toto*, it becomes apparent that in the absence of government, there are inherent imperfections in a staples-oriented development path. First, regional disparities will exist that are themselves variable over time because of unsynchronized instabilities. Second, extraterritorial financing, monopolistic elements, and regional specialization lead to heartland-hinterland exploitation reflected particularly in foreign control. Third, since financial capital is mobile internationally but sticky between industries and since resource augmentation is a private sector decision, multinationals have considerable leverage in dealing with governments. Fourth, a "staples trap" is likely in which domestic financial capital is attracted into minority positions in profitable foreign-controlled firms leading to capital shortages elsewhere. The result is structural distortion.

Many initiatives by the Canadian government – trade protectionism, countercyclical fiscal policies, locational and industry-specific subsidies, supply management – can be seen as attempts to correct or counteract these imperfections. Unfortunately, they have not been altogether successful. Watkins (1978) cites studies in the seventies which show that the dreams of manufacturing self-sufficiency are unfulfilled and that remedial policies are often counter-productive. More recently, various studies undertaken by the Macdonald Commission (Government of Canada 1986) confirm the fact that our inherent imperfections remain entrenched.

In hindsight, it seems that the irony of policy initiatives often overshadows the expected. For example, the National Policy was designed to have a positive and stabilizing impact on economic growth. However, by encouraging foreign firms to locate in central Canada, it also causes regional imbalances that contribute to fiscal deficits and current-account imbalances arising from imported inputs and repatriated rents. The problems are exacerbated further by the imposition of presumably remedial counter-cyclical Keynesian policies. Such policies have two major flaws. First, the initiatives are often directed toward cyclical unemployment when the Canadian problem is structural and regional, so that whereas the private sector has no difficulty absorbing the spoils of budget deficits, it seems incapable of creating the kind of economic environment in which surpluses can be generated. Second, Keynesian theory overestimates both the foresight of Canadian governments and their willingness to discontinue ineffective programs. Questionable expenditures associated with regional development grants, frontier exploration for energy resources, and supply management in agriculture and the fisheries have left the landscape dotted with failed megaprojects and struggling firms. These drains obviously contribute to fiscal deficits but also to current-account deficits because of the servicing costs associated with foreign holdings of our public debt.

These circumstances lead one inexorably to the conclusion that the combination of policy initiatives designed to make us less dependent on staples in fact have had the opposite effect. Because of disarray in both the fiscal and balance of payments accounts, staples activity has to be maintained to provide taxation revenue and export income. Furthermore, the government is hostage to the staples industries, which – to come a full Innisian circle – are controlled by foreign monopolists. The implications of hostageship are disturbing from both a political and an economic perspective but become even more frightening when it is recognized that many of these industries continue to extract depleting resources in ecologically fragile regions.

In some circles, this vulnerability might be taken as evidence of past misjudgments but would not be a signal of potential disaster. It can be argued that in all Western nations, governments are at the mercy of a monopolistic capitalist class who determine the direction of development. While this is true, Canada's situation is atypical because our monopolists have foreign allegiances, and as Grant observes, "No small country can depend for its existence on the loyalty of its capitalists ... Only in dominant nations is the loyalty of capitalists ensured. In such situations, their interests are tied to the strength and vigor of their empire" (Grant 1965, 69). Grant's warning goes unheeded by the present government.

Innis proposed solutions to these problems, focusing on issues such as regional disparities and foreign ownership. If these are conceptualized as conditions on two related dimensions of a bi-polar intellectual framework, it can be seen that structurally the problems are identical in that *both are characterized by domination*, in these cases by the heartland and by multinationals. According to the hypothesis we are seeking to authenticate, the solution would be to work toward a modification of relationships until domination is replaced by tension. In fact, this is what Innis proposed.

His most explicit statements of the proposition are in his later work, where he demonstrates that communications systems shape consciousness in the same way that staples activities shape an economy and that in both realms society benefits if dominating monopolies are replaced by the tensions of competition. The essence of his theory is illustrated by his distinction between spatially and temporally oriented communications systems. The historical roots have been described as follows:

> The media of communications, [Innis] came to believe, were central to the history of organized society and changes in the character of the media meant alterations, often drastic, in institutions, social organizations, and cultural values. Two main classes of media had existed from the beginning of time, each with its different qualities and influences. A heavy, durable medium, such as stone, clay-baked tablets or parchment, emphasized stability, permanence, or time. A light, easily transported material like papyrus or paper meant rapid dissemination over distance or space. A medium of communication that favored time, he believed, emphasized local initiative, respect for antiquity, and religious observance. A space-based medium encouraged secular attitudes, centralized, bureaucratic government, imperialism, and technocracy. (Creighton 1981, 24)

It was Innis's insight that the *idea of progress* has created a regime in which spatially oriented systems have overwhelmed those with a temporal perspective and created a singular "monopoly of knowledge." At the individual level, this condition narrows one's range of exposure and understanding; at the societal level, the monopoly becomes an effective instrument of empire, reinforcing that which is created by the capital flows associated with staples exploitation.

It is possible to use this idea to gain a more insightful understanding of the dynamics of Canadian development. Carey (1981) describes this new outlook. He points out that conventional wisdom characterizes communications media as a liberating force in the development process; it is postulated that true democracy flourishes on the frontier, where in the absence of inherited traditions, indigenous communications systems can bind communities or regions together in a pattern chosen by local residents. Innis purged this theory of its romanticism by showing that, in reality, frontiers are normally dominated by spatially oriented communications monopolies that are instruments used by heartlands to maintain empires.

Thus, to fully appreciate Innis the term monopoly should be given a broad interpretation. It refers not only to the market power of a business firm but to any situation where a single perspective excludes a fundamental opposite. There are monopolies of knowledge, of ideologies, of professional practices, and so on. Innis saw these monoliths as impediments to human fulfilment and believed that it is a government responsibility to introduce an element of competition into their spheres of operation.

Given all this, it can be concluded that Innis's paradigm is consistent with our hypothesized framework. He structures problems and solutions in a way similar to Atwood. He is sensitive to both the dynamics of metamorphosis and the entwining of dimensions. He abhors bias (domination) and encourages balance (tension). Furthermore, he adds hard-core economic dimensions to the framework of local knowledge. Our most visible concerns – fiscal and current account deficits – are surface manifestations of more fundamental forces in a state of disequilibrium: the domination of the margins by the centre, of competitors by monopolists, of nationalists by continentalists, and of time by space. This domination is rooted and reinforced by the activities of both goods-creating industries and consciousness-shaping networks. In short, Innis helps to authenticate the plausibility of the line of reasoning presented in this and the previous chapter.

There are other Innis insights that can help shape a gestalt disciplinary framework. First, his work lends credibility to the notion that the orthodox system is an unsuitable analytical tool because it fails to track the realities of Canadian experience. It has many shortcomings. The assumption that a reasonably consistent growth path can be maintained by market forces ignores the limitations and rhythms imposed by a depletable resource base; the separation of the economic and political realms bifurcates the essence of our reality; as an apostle for spatial orientations, orthodoxy has an inherent bias; it fails to grasp the ubiquity of our monopoly problem and falsely projects that in the absence of intervention, markets will be competitive; it represents heartland, rather than hinterland, interests; it treats the price system as a market-clearing mechanism, rather than a manifestation of the values, institutions, codes of conduct, and authority patterns of society. (See Neill 1972.)

Second, Innis's work also suggests that any new paradigm should have a particularly robust historical component. This approach would allow one to observe the interactions between phenomenal and noumenal forces over time and to catalogue the results of our various attempts to penetrate geographic frontiers, to institutionalize power, to entrench privilege, and to secure personal, community, and national borders. Contemporary mores can then be seen as the residue of these historical acts and the resistances to them. The inclusion of an historical perspective also creates a new series of bi-polar methodological tensions within the discipline, for example, between ascending and decaying institutions and between market efficiency and entropy. Furthermore, it sensitizes the economist both to the pervasiveness of irony and to the fact that all theory, whether pure or gestalt, is prefigured by an ideological position. (See Reinitz 1980 and White 1973.)

Innis also provides us with categories that can be used to undertake analysis within the new paradigm. One which is particularly useful is the concept of empire. With this and an historical perspective, contemporary Canada can be seen as the consequence of the dynamics by which we moved from the British to the American empire while simultaneously erecting our own regional hierarchy. Another Innis category is bias. It might be used to deconstruct and reconstruct social arrangements in a way that is analogous to Marx's approach to the subject of commodity fetishism. For example, one might begin by recognizing that industrial monopolies are manifestations of spatial biases, deconstruct them, then reconstruct them using a criterion embodying a time bias. Out of the contradictions revealed, new policy directions might become apparent. Innis did not see the clash of contending biases as a destructive event, but rather as one that allows intellectuals to escape from narrow modes of thought. In fact, he appears to have been optimistic about the outcome, noting that historically civilizations have been at their peak during periods when they are in transition from one cultural mode to another. It is during such periods that Dennis Lee's metaphorical "savage fields" are most vigorous and creative. (See Lee 1977, 11.)

It is now possible to provide a brief summary of the Innis contribution. He showed that Canada's natural endowments and aspirations are co-mingled to create an economic system characterized by regional disparities, foreign control, and monopolistic industrial structures. Government attempts to solve these problems have been unsuccessful and in fact have added to the burden, with the twin spectre of budgetary and balance of payments deficits. Overlying this is a commitment to the *idea of progress*, initiated and reinforced in our consciousness by a spatially oriented communications network, rooted in the United States. Innis's solution is to replace the monopolies of production and knowledge with competitive arrangements. He provides a detailed model of competition in one dimension – between spatial and time-biased communications systems – but it can be generalized to other spheres so as to become the basis for the research program of a restructured intellectual discipline. This idea is consistent with my own hypothesis. It is also congruent with

Atwood's formulation, with respect to both structure and process. Given this, I now wish to move on and examine the conceptual framework that seems to guide another Canadian humanist.

ALEX COLVILLE

Colville is one of Canada's most distinguished painters. His art expresses a personal philosophy shaped by his own life experiences in this country and not by any overriding commitment to nationalism. This orientation is fortuitous for us because it means that any links between Atwood, Innis, and Colville cannot be dismissed as a polemical collection of ideas from three artists who happen to share the same political philosophy. His work will be analysed at two levels. First, it will be shown that he shares the central tenets of the Atwood-Innis belief system, thereby supporting its authenticity. Second, he has a particular insight that enriches and extends this system.

An attempt to demonstrate that a poet, a political economist, and a painter share common themes, while perhaps unusual in this era of intellectual fragmentation, should not be viewed as a particularly radical exercise. Humanistic theoreticians emphasize the intellectual content of all serious art. That is, "the function of art is not to give the percipient any kind of pleasure, however noble, but to acquaint him with something he had not known before. Art, just like science, aims primarily to be understood." (See Langer 1953, 19.) Thus it should not be surprising that leading artists and social scientists have a common understanding about the elemental conditions of existence even though they approach the problem from different disciplinary perspectives and employ different genres.

As an initial step in understanding Colville, it is helpful to delve briefly into art theory to see what mechanisms painters have at their disposal when seeking to express an idea. Four theoretical concepts need to be understood: a work of art, symbol, semblance, and virtual space. However, there is some imprecision in the literature as to how these terms should be defined. Hence it is prudent to use a single reference to ensure internal consistency; Langer (1953) has been chosen as that reference.

A *work of art* is something that expresses an idea about the human condition in its physical and/or metaphysical dimensions. A good work of art is one in which the understood idea is plausible and cogent and the piece is skilfully crafted, given the standards of the day. There are innumerable cogent ideas about the human condition and each art form is suited to explore a particular subset of these. For example, the tonal structures of music can be made to conform to the dynamics of emotive life and to symbolize patterns of growth and attenuation, conflict and resolution, excitement and calm. Discursive literature is most appropriate for explaining aspects of the domain of experience that are amenable to logic or where the causal relationships are complex and tangled. Poetry is suitable where human feeling is so intense that it can best be captured by metaphor. The forte of visual art is to use shapes, colours, and juxtapositions to capture relationships at a moment in time but also to involve the percipient to the extent that he feels compelled to reflect about the dynamics. Exceptional visual art moves these mentations toward the contemplation of ideas that are within the domains of other art forms. Colville produces exceptional works of art.

A work of art expresses its fundamental ideas symbolically. A *symbol* is any device used to make an abstraction. That is, an object, relationship, movement, or sequence is chosen to represent some other phenomenon, which is usually intangible and complex. For example, a flag or a national anthem – a simple piece of cloth to be seen and a simple sequence of tones to be heard – represents the intricately complex idea of statehood and thus is a symbol.

Visual pictorial art presents an image as a symbol. Further, a painting is a single undivided symbol, a fact that is often obscured by the vacuous distinction between form and content. The various elements and relationships are not meant to guide our thoughts to something tangible they resemble but to the idea that they symbolize. Unfortunately, many of us think of an image as something visual and this attitude places a conceptual limit on our interpretation. That is, the word "image" is almost inseparably wedded to the sense of sight, when in fact the work may be symbolizing an idea for whose comprehension other senses, feelings, and the intellect may be required.

Fortunately there are other words that escape this narrow visual association, one of which is Jung's term *semblance*. His exemplary case of semblance is the dream, where sounds, smells, feelings, intentions, and ideas – all sorts of intangible elements – interact with sight. Because the concept of semblance liberates perceptions, it enhances the power of conception. The viewer is encouraged to disengage from his own attachment to the practical functions of the elements in the painting and move toward an unconstrained gestalt interpretation of the ideas they symbolize. "The function of 'semblance' is to give forms a new embodiment in purely qualitative, unreal instances, setting them free from their normal embodiment in real things so that they can be recognized in their own right, and freely conceived and composed in the interest of the artist's ultimate aim – significance "(Langer 1953, 50). In some ways, the creation and use of semblance is analogous to the process already noted in the work of Marx (e.g., commodity fetishism) and Innis (e.g., use of bias as an elemental unit of analysis) in which there is deconstruction followed by reconstruction and reinterpretation. With semblance, each element is estranged from its practical life and endowed with benign self-sufficiency. It then becomes a unit in reconstruction and is set in a relationship with other elements so as to replicate the logical structure of the ideas being symbolized. But the process of reconstruction has a monstrous limitation that paradoxically presents the greatest scope for artistic ingenuity and craftsmanship: because of the pictorial form, all relationships must be reduced to the visual and the static. That is, there must be fixed visual substitutes for those aspects of ideas that are normally understood through the non-visual senses, feelings, or movement. In the end, the final artistic symbol may be intricate in the extreme, connecting the rational and emotive relationships between all the elements that are relevant to the idea being expressed. Yet it must be simple enough to be understood. The layman is fortunate that Colville is a realistic painter because his elements serve as descriptors as well as symbols.

Thus, the final object on the wall, the painting, is not experiential space but *virtual space*. It exists for vision alone but transmits non-visual ideas through geometric arrangements, spatial juxtapositions, attitudes, textures, colours, and tones. The painting is a metaphor for an idea or a complex of ideas, of which there is an immense range of possibilities. As with other art forms, it can relate to the visible world and/or inquire into the mysteries of the unconscious; it can be cast within a romantic, comic, tragic, or satirical mode; it can be based in a particular ideological position or explain aspects of eternal verities such as love, beauty, or trust. Our task is to examine how Colville uses virtual space.

In my view, most of Colville's paintings have a common set of characteristics:

• Each painting has two primary elements held in opposition to each other.
• Each element is given the same degree of attention; one does not dominate the other.
• The themes emphasize human relationships, civilization and nature, center-margin distinctions, and space-time interactions.
• The cogent ideas spring from the relationships between the elements. It is one of tension, and the symbolic contribution of each

element can only be understood if this tension is incorporated into its definition.

• In virtual space there is therefore an element of dissonance because the definition of each element incorporates relational considerations from an opposing element.

If these points can be demonstrated, they tend to authenticate the bi-polar framework being posited, as well as the reasonableness of attaching primacy to the dimensions identified by Atwood and Innis.

There is little doubt that dualities constitute a fundamental feature of Colville's art. This is evidenced by their titles: *Boat and Marker, Cat and Artist, Church and Horse, Crow and Calf, Cyclist and Crow, Dog and Bridge, Dog and Priest, Family and Rainstorm, Horse and Train, Nude and Dummy, Seeing-Eye Dog and Man, Target Pistol and Man, Woman and Terrier*. Moreover, it is not difficult to show that subject matter often parallels the dimensions of the Atwood-Innis belief systems. Many examples are available and often a single picture portrays a multiplicity of themes. Six will be mentioned, the first three as illustrations of a primary theme and the latter three to illustrate more complicated thematic arrangements. (See plates.)

Couple on Beach contrasts the bearings of the two sexes. He is uneasy and restless, gazing toward the horizon oblivious to the natural and sensuous beauty within his touch. His posture displays a desire to dominate space by penetration and his partner by neglect, but there is no evidence of success. She is adaptive. She accepts the pleasant warmth of the sand with her body and rejects the cruel heat of the sun's glare with her hat. She is turned to express a willingness; he is hunched to express a will.

Horse and Train contrasts the imperatives of technology and nature. The train is a leviathan of steel; its ordained path is defined by the rails that guide it to its destination, its way foretold by an uncompromising light beam. The horse gallops freely and intuitively, indifferent to the structures that rational man has constructed even though they are potentially lethal. Will the horse swerve and acknowledge the superiority of technology? Can intervention prevent disaster?

Nude and Dummy captures the essence of the relationship between the centre and the margin. The dummy at the centre of the room and the picture establishes the standard by which conformity is defined and expectations are signalled. The dummy is authority. The woman at the edge of the room is unusually beautiful and exudes confidence. Nevertheless, she is expected to conform to the dictates

Alex Colville *Couple on Beach* 1957
National Gallery of Canada, Ottawa

Alex Colville *Horse and Train* 1954
Glazed tempera on masonite, 41.2 × 54.2 cm
Art Gallery of Hamilton
Gift of Dominion Foundries and Steel Ltdf. (Dofasco Inc.), 1957

Alex Colville *Nude and Dummy* 1950
New Brunswick Museum, Saint John

of the dummy. Her look embodies both scepticism and quietude, a mood that typifies existence at the margin.

Professor of Romance Languages is a masterful statement of tensions between space and time, modernity and tradition, and rationalism and imaginative reflection. The factory with a smokestack stretching toward the heavens spews smoke to the horizon. It is the embodiment of the spatial domination associated with industrialism. The professor is the personification of tradition. His clothes, glasses, moustache, baldness, gaze, and demeanour are of a piece. He lives in a world of ideas from another culture. Whatever may be the subject of his thoughts, it is unlikely to be related to factories. Yet the two primary elements in the picture not only coexist but recognize that their own integrity is conditional on the integrity of their fundamental opposite.

To Prince Edward Island is another complex ensemble of ideas. Visually, the two most prominent elements are the woman and an array of very worthwhile technological artifacts: the boat itself, which allows her to widen her experiences spatially; the lifeboat, the rail, and the fence, which provide security; the binoculars, which extend her senses and give forewarning about conditions at the destination. However, the tension in the painting is at a less obvious level: between the woman and the man. In contrast to her inquisitiveness, he observes the destination and the seascape with patience and a more relaxed perspective. He sees something different from what she does and is not discontent: his extension is the result of mentation rather than technology. There is also tension at another level because the binoculars are focused directly at the viewer. It is difficult to avoid being jolted into an uncomfortable involvement, a discomfort that can only be resolved by inquiry. (See Kroker 1985.)

Berlin Bus is another painting with a multiplicity of themes. Perhaps the dominant one parallels the central idea in *Horse and Train*: the tension between technology and nature. The force of technology is evident in the bus, in the advertisements and signs announcing the availability of infrastructure, and in numerous other components of a modern urban street. The woman is the epitome of natural energy, an array of limbs which though seemingly unco-ordinated are effectively moving her through space. However, the arrangement initiates a complex array of questions. Why does she run? Is she striving to catch the bus or demonstrating her independence? Is she celebrating her refusal to be overwhelmed? Or does she symbolize a warning about the technological monolith? Burnett attaches primacy to the latter issue. He states,

[The] three elements, notary, bus, advertisement, are all embodiments of social and institutional values. The maintenance of the structure of modern society depends on the orderly and regulated conveyance of goods, services and people, whether in transport, the law, or in the communication of information and opinion. Between these the girl runs with a frantic nightmarish energy, as if trying to break free from some unnameable threat. It is as if she alone is aware of something terrible, of a world whose order and efficiency, marked even in the precise placing of paving stones, could at any moment split apart. (Burnett 1983, 133)

However, whatever the interpretation, one is forced to examine the duplicity of both technology and the spirit of nature, as well as the tensions between them. There are also secondary oppositional themes present in the painting. The east-west duality of Berlin itself and the mental anguish Colville is said to have felt in living there a generation after his war experiences are examples. Further, one might detect an Atwood type of sexual tension between male as technology and woman as free spirit. Burnett also sees a tension between the rational conscious and the presumably irrational subconscious.

The nightmarish character of the picture cuts into levels at which all of us exist. It is like the way a dream breaks through the rationalizing structure of the conscious, serving to show how we exist at different levels of reality. The fact that the girl here is "out of place" is relative only to the expectations we construct for our conscious and everyday levels. The dream world is no less real, carrying its own time and space, which, if different from the objective world, is in no way rendered invalid by it. (Burnett 1983, 134)

When these six paintings are considered *in toto*, they are seen to exhibit a common pattern. In each, there are two primary oppositional elements and the cogent idea is carried by the relationship between them. This relationship is one of mutual tension, which itself takes on different forms. In some it is latent and implied, for one wonders about the dynamics of coexistence between the man and the woman in both *Couple on the Beach* and *To Prince Edward Island*; in one painting it is savage, for the horse's fate may be brutal; one is ambivalent, for the margin's interaction with the centre is itself duplicitous; one is eternal, for space and time intersect but never coalesce; one is cerebral, for there is uncertainty as to whether the woman will use the bus or remain free spirited. But in all cases, each element is unwilling to sacrifice its own integrity in spite of the pull from its fundamental opposite. Acquiescence is not a motif in Colville's work.

The similarity between the themes of Atwood, Innis, and Colville is obvious. There is, however, an interesting difference. The former two tend to dwell on relationships involving domination whereas Colville is less likely to do so. This fact is ironic because Colville is identified as a realistic painter, but of the three, he may be the most idealistic.

However, there is another aspect of Colville's work that links him to Atwood and Innis and that helps to clarify some of the ideas with which they are grappling. It will be recalled that Atwood seeks to instil meaning into apparently ambiguous situations (e.g., as in the *Journals*) and Innis is engaged in the process of deconstruction so that new meanings can be attached to social processes. Colville is similarly engaged in the quest for meaning. His contribution arises from the fact that the ideas he seeks to articulate invariably include a dissonant component because each element can only be defined in the context of its opposite. To take a simple example, in *Horse and Train* neither element is a meaningful symbol by itself: they only transmit a cogent idea in juxtaposition.

What this characteristic implies is that dissonance must be confronted rather than avoided if one is to discover the truth. While this concept has been alluded to in reviewing Atwood's work, the visual art form brings it into sharper relief. It is an immensely important idea, and tragically Western man has been conditioned to act otherwise. Normally we interpret dissonance to be incoherence and structure our decision criteria and intellectual strategies around a framework in which it is not included. As a result, our decisions are often misguided and our searches are unrewarded because we have failed to understand the essence of the problem we seek to resolve.

The insight sheds light on Lee's observation that "the civil self seeks nourishment, as much as the biological self ... if everything it can find is *alien*, it may protect itself in a visceral spasm of refusal" (Lee 1974, 162, italics added). Dissonance is *alien* to the citizen immersed in a society devoted to pursuit of the *idea of progress*. It is interpreted to be in the realm of the incomprehensible, and there is a refusal to acknowledge its existence. Out of the cacophonous tangle of reality the apparently harmonious threads that represent modernity are grasped for guidance. Civilization is given precedence over nature, reason over intuition, space over time, self over community, order over disorder. By severing the tense relationship between these polarities, one also severs the opportunity to comprehend the truth.

It has been said about Atwood that she has a "desire for a more inclusive life reconciling hitherto unmanageable complexities," about Innis that his work was grounded in the application of the principle which can be termed "perspective by incongruity," and about Colville that the essential character of his work is the belief that "ambiguity is ... not a barrier to understanding but rather is its condition." There is common ground here that provides an insight about the essence of Canada's local knowledge.

Alex Colville *Professor of Romance Languages* 1973
Mr and Mrs Irving Ungerman

Alex Colville *To Prince Edward Island* 1965
National Gallery of Canada, Ottawa

Alex Colville *Berlin Bus* 1978
Private collection, Montreal

5 The Method

Opposition is true friendship.

If Foucault's strategy for disciplinary reform has merit, if universal knowledge is adequately represented by the ontological theories of Blake, Kierkegaard, and Tillich, if Canada's local knowledge is captured by the ideas of Atwood, Innis, and Colville, and if academics are genuinely interested in the pursuit of truth, it follows that Canada's economics discipline should be based on a dialectic methodology. The objectives of this chapter are to demonstrate the veracity and implications of this conclusion.

The first task is simple. It has been shown that both universal and local knowledge have dialectic structures, and since a gestalt intellectual discipline should be patterned in the same way as the reality it seeks to analyse, economics too should be dialectical.

However, it is a much more difficult task to determine the implications of adopting such a methodology, because dialectics is a very elusive concept. Its history goes back to classical Greece and to its founder, Heraclitus, who rebelled against Pythagorean dualism (i.e., that all things are composed of independent contraries) by arguing that the contraries are inseparable and form a dynamic unity. Through the centuries a Heraclitean school of thought has persisted, but in the present era it has been overshadowed by the *idea of progress* perspective, which gives primacy to reason and verifiability rather than to the contraries of existence.

There are at least two fundamental reasons why the concept of the dialectic is so evanescent. First, it has been applied to an immense range of seemingly unrelated topics. Some writers use it to explain the unfolding of history, others to search for the laws and principles of metaphysical existence. For some it is a preferred method of argumentation in the pursuit of truth, while for others its value is analytical rather than rhetorical. To some it is a positive concept, while to others it is most useful for normative evaluation. Furthermore, it has been utilized from a variety of different disciplinary perspectives. Theologians see it as a means of explaining the unity between man and god; philosophers use it as a basis for establishing the relationship between subject and object and between reason and unreason; social scientists see it as a useful device for describing community processes. Each application introduces a new range of nuances, elaborations, and definitions, and in this diffusion, consistency and clarity are often sacrificed.

But there is a second and perhaps more compelling reason why there seems to be such a jumble of dialectic threads in Western thought. The dialectic is the tool of the humanist, and each practitioner brings his or her own intellectual baggage along when constructing a work of art. This prefiguring makes it difficult to compare two dialecticians even when they seek to communicate essentially the same idea. The issue is further complicated by the fact that because of the subject matter, conclusions are normally evaluated in terms of plausibility and aesthetics rather than scientific proof. For these reasons, ambiguity and argument cannot be expunged from dialectic analysis. An excellent example is provided by White (1973), who contrasts the theories of two of the most formidable dialecticians, Hegel and Marx, and concludes that they each prefigured reality in terms of their own poetic vision and hence neither theory can be refuted. Nevertheless, there seems to be a core *method* by which dialectic analysis should proceed, regardless of the topic. Israel (1979) has provided a clear statement of what is involved.

Dialectic analysis is a process that emerges out of an understanding of its four basic categories: totality, intrinsic relations, process, and relatedness. A preliminary definition of what these categories entail can be obtained by describing what each negates. The category of totality negates the ideas of dualism and atomism; the category of intrinsic relations negates extrinsic relations; the category of process negates the notion of static constancy and equilibrium; the category of relatedness negates the treatment of social facts as independent data. Given these definitions, the categories and the relationships between them can be examined.

TOTALITY

Totality implies that one should treat opposites as a unity and eventually that one should perceive the whole social arrangement as a composite of such unities. However, to accomplish this goal, one must transpose empirical concreteness into thought concreteness, again by a process of deconstruction and reconstruction. The process can be explained as follows. We are interested in studying reality, so we direct our attention to the subject matter of our inquiry, say a range of normal human activities. However, as man does not normally reflect about the deeper meaning of routine activities, they only have a loosely and unsystematically organized empirical concreteness. A dialectic analysis requires that the various elements in the activity be isolated or abstracted from each other. They are then recombined in the context of their oppositional qualities so as to constitute a new interpretation of the original activities, now expressed in terms of thought concreteness. Marx gives an example of what is involved.

It seems to be the correct procedure to commence with the real and concrete aspect of conditions as they are; in the case of political economy, to commence with population which is the basis and the author of the entire productive activity of society. Yet, on closer consideration it proves to be wrong. Population is an abstraction, if we leave out e.g. the classes of which it consists. These classes, again, are but an empty word, unless we know what are the elements on which they are based, such as wage – labor, capital, etc. ... If we start out, therefore, with population, we do so with a chaotic conception of the whole, and by closer analysis we will gradually arrive at simpler ideas ... This once attained, we might start on our return journey until we would finally come back to population, but this time not as a chaotic notion of an integral whole, but as a rich aggregate of many conceptions and relations. (Marx 1913, 292)

While there is no guarantee that the process necessarily leads to a rich aggregate, there are many examples of situations where the penetration of distortions caused by surface appearance leads to the discovery of essences. For example, Innis's attempt to understand monopolies by reducing them to networks of biased communications systems is a transition from empirical surface concreteness to an abstraction that is then used to reconstruct an essential thought concreteness. Colville's use of pictorial elements to portray abstract symbols that then become components of a cogent idea follows a similar pattern.

Furthermore, there are several noteworthy characteristics of this concept of totality that help to distinguish the dialectic method from the intellectual orientation embodied in the *idea of progress*. For example, because the essential knowledge contained in thought concreteness is produced by reflection, the method is contrary to empiricism. While it does resemble that employed by Descartes (i.e., both reject sense data), here too there is a fundamental difference: the dialectician substitutes a world of oppositional relationships whereas the Cartesian substitutes a world of mathematical relationships. Furthermore, because of the concentration on totalities, the idea of atomism that led to the creation of *economic man* is also rejected. Finally, the fact that essential knowledge is *produced* by human effort has important implications. By drawing attention to the fact that the social arrangement is also a man-made creation and that empirical concreteness may be detrimental to the functioning of the mechanisms contained in thought concreteness, it encourages intervention. In short, the dialectic method rejects empiricism, rationalism, and atomism but fosters involvement (i.e., praxis) rather than mere analysis.

INTRINSIC RELATIONS

For a totality to be designated as dialectic, certain relationships must exist between the polar elements, or *relata*, contained therein. Paramount among these is that they must be different yet interdependent, a condition captured by the term *intrinsic*. If one develops an understanding of what this concept implies, it is then possible to become more precise about the oppositional and dynamic characteristics of dialectic relationships.

First, let us examine its negation: an extrinsic relationship. This term describes a relationship that does not alter the relata, either in how they are defined or in how they are able to function. It is the idea inferred in elementary statistical analysis by which discrete variables are correlated without losing their autonomy. However, in an intrinsic relationship, the relata lose their independence and attain new meaning through conjunction, as in the following example. "A watch is placed on the table and all its parts are separated and displaced. The relation between each of the parts is extrinsic in the spatial sense. Then we join them such that the watch can function. The parts become intrinsically related to each other" (Israel 1979, 83).

It is the existence of intrinsic relationships that gives the dialectic method its elusiveness because the condition cannot be easily accommodated within more orthodox conceptual arrangements such as that which is embodied in the *idea of progress*. However, this characteristic shifts the controversy to another level because it inevitably leads to disputes as to whether a particular relationship is intrinsic or extrinsic. For example, there is disagreement amongst linguists about the relationship between language and social reality. Another example that is more germane to my own analysis is the relationship which exists between technology and man. Indeed, the whole line of reasoning presented in this book is predicated on the proposition that that relationship is intrinsic; if it is not, the argument crumbles as well as the suitability of the dialectic method as a tool for analysing economic processes. Given this, it is prudent to discuss the technology-man relationship briefly, in order to reinforce the authenticity of the larger argument that is being developed as well as to provide an example of what is meant by intrinsic.

The issues involved in the controversy are described by Hood (1972), who focuses on two main protagonists: Aristotle and Heidegger. Aristotle believed that technology was extrinsic, taking the view that it involves the production of objects which are neither necessary nor natural but are created to provide security, comfort, pleasure, and the like, and as such are strictly instrumental. Having created these objects, we human beings are free to pursue nobler objectives and to realize the potential of our existence more fully. For example, we have more opportunity to search for the truth, devise rules of proper conduct, and design optimal forms of government. Thus, there is a hierarchy of activities, and technology is one of the lower forms. It does not define man's nobler purposes or impede in their realization. A man may use a hammer for his own purposes, but they remain independent entities and there is no transcendence in their relationship. They are extrinsic to each other.

Heidegger condemns this conceptualization as being trivial and misleading. He argues that there is a fundamental error in the belief that man is endowed with a preordained and immutable hierarchy of activities. Rather, he is a relational creature who formulates his system of values and activities in response to his everyday experiences. Technology shapes these experiences in a multitude of ways: nature is seen as a reservoir of resources and energy; work and its significance are defined according to a technical imperative; community structures are adjusted according to its dictates. Hence it also shapes the hierarchy. Technology and man bear an intrinsic relationship to each other. The illusion that they do not, as suggested by the man-hammer example, is a false interpretation because it fails to recognize that the hammer is only a small component in a larger technological apparatus which has allowed man to transcend his primitive or pre-primitive state. Grant's analysis of the statement that "the computer does not impose on us the ways in which it should be used" reaches a similar conclusion.

To the extent that Heidegger's line of reasoning is persuasive, it illustrates what is meant by an intrinsic relationship and also tends to confirm the reasonableness of the theories of determinism sum-marized in chapter two. Furthermore, it gives substance to a per-spective that was identified with Colville. The dissonance that is seen to exist in his definitions can be interpreted to be a particular con-ceptualization of intrinsic relationships.

In any case, all dialectic relationships are intrinsic. In addition, they must be oppositional in one of three ways: they may be mutually exclusive and exhaustive, mutually exclusive but not exhaustive, or complementary but converse. Before providing examples of each cat-egory, it is helpful to identify two other characteristics of oppositional relata. First, since social processes involve many oppositions or con-tradictions, single relata can be involved in more than one relation-ship simultaneously. For analytical purposes it simplifies matters if these can be identified as either primary or secondary, although the distinction is sometimes arbitrary. However, the simultaneity means that there is a network of opposites so that the totality which is defined as the subject matter of a particular analysis can be con-nected to the larger totality that constitutes the whole social environ-ment. In this way, dialectic opposites become the links that bind various components of reality into a comprehensive gestalt theory. Second, the opposites need not be symmetrical for one can dominate the other. This is a point of great importance, and I will return to it later, after providing some illustrations of the various categories that have just been identified.

An example of a mutually exclusive and exhaustive opposite is that which exists between men and women. Use of this example also helps to bring Atwood's work into sharper focus because her feminist work can now be seen as a lament that the relationship between the sexes is most often extrinsic or imperfectly intrinsic (because it involves domination), rather than intrinsic and transcendent. An example of a mutually exclusive, but non-exhaustive, dialectic rela-tionship is one between dictatorship and democracy; it is non-exhaus-tive simply because other forms of government are also possible. An example of a complementary, but converse, relationship is a market transaction between a buyer and a seller. When it occurs in an ideal world of perfect competition, it is symmetrical; when it occurs in the real world of monopoly power, it involves domination. Hence Innis's theories of monopoly are amenable to dialectic analysis.

However, a dialectic relationship must not only be intrinsic and oppositional, it must also be dynamic, because the various relata are in a continual state of flux. As circumstances are modified, so also are the binding forces. Indeed, many of those who use the dialectic method to explain history attach primacy to situations in which a relationship involving domination is challenged and explain social change as the consequence of such challenges. It is this type of dynamic aspect that makes an understanding of process a central feature of dialectic methodology.

PROCESS

Process refers to the continuum of forces that operate in the time-space dimension of a particular totality and that result in some form of transformation of the totality. The forces result from the symbiotic interaction between human activity (praxis) and natural entropic decay. Process is a familiar concept in orthodox economics, where the distinction between stocks (structures) and flows (process) is commonplace. However, because of its emphasis on comparative statics and equilibrium, orthodoxy tends to emphasize stocks, whereas in dialectic reasoning, primacy is attached to flows and stocks are viewed merely as the instantaneous manifestation of underlying processes, as illustrated, for example, by the photograph in Atwood's poetry. While this difference is subtle and one of degree rather than kind, it can have a significant effect on how one perceives a totality or seeks to modify its trajectory.

Process can involve growth, decay, metamorphosis, or inversion. This last possibility deserves elucidation because it is virtually unknown in orthodoxy but of central importance in dialectics. Hegel's analysis of the master-slave relationship provides the classic example.

Hegel starts with the proposition that individuals need recognition but that it is only meaningful if it is bestowed by someone considered to be an equal or a superior; recognition by a perceived inferior is a non-event. In this context, a master-slave relationship is one involving superiority and inferiority. The master dominates because he controls the means of production; the slave is subservient but must participate in the productive process if he is to survive. However, the master gets no utility out of any recognition that might emanate from the slave; his recognition must come from his peer group, with whom he must compete in a manner that Veblen later refers to as conspicuous consumption. Within this group, as one desire is satisfied it is replaced by another because conspicuous consumption is addictive. The master becomes the slave of his own insatiability.

Simultaneously, in his role as a producer, the slave is developing his own skills and becoming aware that he is able to control his natural environment. Within his own realm, he has become a master.

In short, an inversion has occurred. The slave's praxis has increased his awareness of his own potentialities, whereas that of the master has turned him into a slave.

The implications of inversion are truly profound and boundless. Marx used the concept to explain alienation, reification, the inevitability of social unrest, and the ironic destructiveness of a class society. In addition, he saw it as an insightful way of illustrating the intimate relationship between human beings and their work. To quote him, "The outstanding achievement of Hegel's *Phenomenology* and of its final outcome, the dialectic of negativity as the moving and generating principle, is ... that Hegel conceives the self-creation of man as a process ... that he thus grasps the essence of labor and comprehends objective man ... as the outcome of man's own labor" (Marx 1964, 177). Thus a dialectic interpretation of work is dramatically different from the orthodox view, in which it is a necessary evil whose value is determined by the wage rate. To the dialectician, it should be a means of fulfilment and authentic socialization and should be organized accordingly. As indicated earlier, this view is comparable to that expressed by Blake two centuries ago and articulated by John Paul II (1981) and Schumacher (1973) more recently.

But inversion also provides a promising conceptual basis for interpreting many other aspects of reality. For example, it can be applied to the technology-man relationship that is so central to the line of reasoning in this study. Human beings originally developed technology to serve their own ends, but an inversion has occurred and now, as Emerson observed tersely, "things are in the saddle and ride mankind." Furthermore, we can take our understanding one step further by noting that there can be relationships between two different inversions. For example, technology-man intersects with master-slave. In recent years, we have seen that technology has become a potent preference-shaping force, primarily as a result of innovations in electronic communications systems and the shift from aversive to positive control mechanisms. This change has resulted in a situation in which wage-labour, the contemporary analogue of slaves, has adopted the mentality of its master, the managerial and capitalist class, and is correspondingly enslaved by its own insatiability.

One final example of inversion should be mentioned. It will be recalled that in "Progressive Insanities of the Pioneer" Atwood describes how an attempt to conquer nature results in a reversal in which man is himself conquered. This is an instance of an avoidable inversion taken from Canada's local knowledge.

In any case, the shift in emphasis from structure to process means that praxis becomes a central category of dialectic analysis. This focus on human action means that in economics, one concentrates on human beings' role as producers, consumers, and shapers of institutional arrangements which themselves bear dialectic relationships to each other. But the function of production and consumption is vastly different from that in the orthodox paradigm, where it is the value of goods which is of prime concern. In the dialectic framework, primacy is attached to the effect of praxis on people themselves and on the extent to which it aids them in the process of transcendence.

RELATEDNESS

It is customary to make a distinction between the physical world and the social world. Orthodox disciplines treat these as separate phenomena, creating dualisms in both the real world and the world of knowledge, and often a secondary dualism as, for example, when intellectuals construct pure, rather than gestalt, theories. Orthodox economics is guilty of further bifurcation because of its atomistic axiom structure and its tendency to perceive its field of inquiry in terms of extrinsic relationships between variables.

In dialectics the whole complex is seen as a totality that is bound together by praxis. In the physical world the praxis culminates in the creation of the technological apparatus; in the intellectual world, in the creation of theories; and in the social world, in the creation of institutional arrangements. However, if one starts to analyse, say, Canada as an empirically concrete totality and as a first step abstracts it into relata such as the technological apparatus and the capitalistic system, it is immediately apparent that the relata themselves are enormously complex relationships. For example, the capitalistic system can be seen as a set of relationships between the economy and the superstructure; in turn, the economy can be perceived as relationships between units producing various kinds of commodities, obtaining inputs from various sources, and operating in various kinds of competitive environments; the superstructure is composed of an array of government agencies with fiscal and regulative mandates interacting with a variety of social groupings. That is to say, the original relata – in this case, the capitalistic system – is itself a relationship that is amenable to further abstraction. This characteristic can be referred to as *relatedness*, and the dialectic method requires that this further abstraction be undertaken to reveal underlying intrinsic relationships with their various opposites and

dynamics. Having accomplished this result, the process of constructing a thought concreteness can commence in which reality is
now perceived as an interactive process whereby "each relation ...
produces transformations of those relations to which it is related and
through them, to other relations." (See Israel 1979, 128.)

Nevertheless, a fundamental methodological dilemma remains.
Specifically, how far should one continue to abstract and go on dis-
aggregating relata into relationships? One cannot continue forever in
a process of infinite regression, so a basic unit of dialectic analysis
must somehow be identified. This is the problem of *individuation*,
and there is not unanimity as to how it should be addressed. However, Marx's solution seems to be the most plausible where he argues
that man himself should be the basic unit so long as he is viewed as
"an ensemble of social relationships." It is necessary to exercise great
care in interpreting this phrase, particularly the two words *social* and
relationships.

In German the word used when talking about something societal
is *gesellschaftlich*. As Israel (1979, 139) points out, it has two different
meanings. One refers to generic relations such as those between
capital and labour, citizen and government, or male values and female
values; the other refers to specific individual relations such as the
one between me and my grandchild. It is the former that is of primary
concern to the social scientist because analysis obviously becomes
too unwieldy if it is concerned with every person X relating to person
Y in place Z at time T. This is not to say that the dialectic method is
not valuable for explaining individual social relations; Atwood and
others have shown its great potential. However, given the present
state of dialectic analysis in the social sciences, generic considerations
should probably take precedence over individual ones. With respect
to abstraction through relatedness, the problem is not so much where
to stop, but rather how to begin.

The second word, *relationship*, is not ambiguous but is emphasized
because it carries great significance. People are no longer seen in
terms of traits or attributes but as an embodiment of process. They
are the result of the relationships initiated by their own praxis.
However, even though the unit of analysis is the individual, the
analysis penetrates to the conscious and subconscious aspects of his
or her existence.

Thus the human being, seen as an ensemble of social relations,
becomes the basic unit of dialectic analysis, and the discovery of
relatedness becomes the means by which he or she is revealed. It
is in such discoveries that the creative artistry of the dialectician
is demonstrated. Marx is recognized as the grand master and his

analyses of commodity fetishism, reification of labour, and commodity values are universally admired, even if somewhat grudgingly by proponents of orthodoxy. But the effect of the creativity has a common theme: through relatedness one is able to transform apparently static constructs of the physical and social worlds into relations and hence into process.

Since relatedness and process presuppose each other and since neither can be understood without acknowledging the categories of totality and intrinsic relations, the four categories of the dialectic method themselves constitute an intrinsically related, dynamic totality. Because of this fact one can say that it is truly a gestalt formulation. Just as it seeks to redefine reality, it seeks to redefine the intellectual processes normally used to comprehend that reality.

These four categories comprise the framework for the dialectic method. Put briefly, one transforms empirical concreteness into thought concreteness through abstraction in which the dynamic aspects of intrinsic oppositional relationships are first revealed and then combined. In the end, one normally comprehends existence to be much more complex and intricate than originally perceived.

However, the method is not a panacea and it is wise to point out some of its limitations. Some critics have argued that it is counterintuitive, but often this criticism merely means that it is counter to the thought processes inculcated by the *idea of progress*. It is difficult to grasp webs of change, totality, and the unity of opposites when one has been conditioned to think in terms of equilibrium, atomism, and extrinsic relationships. Others contend that it has limited predictive powers. While this argument is true, it must also be admitted that the track record of orthodox economics is less than exemplary even when it has a superstructure working to turn its predictions into actualities. A more penetrating criticism is that the dialectic method violates the rules of accepted scientific procedure based on the formulation of refutable hypothesis. While this claim is also true, the dialectic procedure is defensible because it has a different objective from orthodox science. It seeks to discover real essences by penetrating through the systematic distortions imposed on us by industrial society, whereas the orthodox scientist seeks to discover regularities by penetrating through what are perceived to be random disturbances.

The dialectic method emerges relatively unscathed from these kinds of criticisms. However, it does have its Achilles heel.

The difficulty arises when we seek the [means] to implement the [method] – the specific instructions, the algorithms, the handbook of instructions for realizing each step along the road toward abstraction and back to concreteness. For then we discover that crucially important decisions must be made at each stage – deciding which abstract element to pursue, disentangling "decisive" connections from accidental ones, specifying the process of analysis or reconstitution, judging the final result for its usefulness. (Heilbroner 1980, 45)

While the dialectic method is an art form without a prescribed analogue, we are not left in a morass of intellectual anarchy. We do have some direction: the totalities and categories to be analysed have been identified by Blake, Kierkegaard, and Tillich and by Atwood, Innis, and Colville; we know that within these categories, the objective of praxis is to preserve tension; we have the experiences of some grand masters, which can be used as models to provide inspiration about how to proceed. In this latter regard, it is useful to examine Marx briefly.

First, it is appropriate to make a few general comments about Marx's work. As is well understood, he derived his theoretical system from Hegel, transforming the mentor's spiritual orientation – in which dialectic historical processes would eventually bring the German state into communion with God – into one anchored in materialism. Further, he shifted his position on the dialectic as he matured. In his earlier work (e.g., *Thesis on Feuerback*) Marx urged active intervention to create social change; later (e.g., *Capital*) he sought to reveal the underlying dialectic laws according to which advanced capitalism would inevitably be transformed into socialism. These two phases are sometimes referred to as critical and scientific Marxism. (See Gouldner 1980 and Jay 1984.) The former concentrates on humanistic, romantic, and consciousness-raising praxis; the latter emphasizes a gradualistic, evolutionary, technological agenda. Both have some relevance to the contemporary Canadian scene, although, perhaps paradoxically, an examination of the scientific theory is particularly instructive.

The essence of Marx's scientific theory is unambiguous and also well known. Empirically concrete capitalism is projected through a thought concrete process to become socialism. Because this evolution has not occurred, orthodox economists tend to dismiss Marx as being irrelevant. However, a dialectic reasoner might not be so intransigent but rather see the merit of reworking the analysis to discover which processes Marx failed to anticipate and how they have deflected revolutionary praxis. Why is it that industrial societies such as Canada tolerate high levels of unemployment, unchanging and unequal distribution of income, unfulfilling work patterns, and dehumanizing technology with scarcely a murmur of revolutionary praxis?

The most obvious explanation is that class consciousness has failed to materialize. But what has thwarted its emergence? Here Skinner's explanation of social processes provides a clue. It will be recalled that he argues that the underlying theme which has guided industrial civilization has been the replacement of aversive control mechanisms by positive ones. In recent years this shift has been particularly effective because the technological apparatus has been designed specifically to shape preferences to conform to the needs of the capitalist class. That is to say, the predicted dialectic between capitalist and labour has been replaced by one between determinism and free will.

The emergence of a revolutionary praxis in Canada has also been deterred by government policies because the major thrust of fiscal, monetary, and regulatory activities has been to generate employment. Unfortunately, the price has been high: a declining resource base, environmental degradation, foreign ownership, and massive debts. But debts have to be repaid. In this case, much of the burden will fall on future generations of Canadians, who will face triple jeopardy because they will have to do so within the limitations imposed by declining resource rents and a threatened environment.

Thus class conflict in the present has been prevented by taxing future generations. Two comments about this state of affairs seem appropriate. First, it seems immoral to tax those who are unrepresented. Second, this interpretation adds substance to the time-space imbalances identified by Atwood and Innis.

What these comments suggest is that a scientific Marxian analysis yields great insights into the Canadian social arrangement as long as one is asking the correct question: why did the revolution fail? The simple answer is that his categories were not correctly specified. The more instructive answer is that class consciousness was deflected by introducing two new dialectic relationships in which determinism dominates free will and the present dominates the future. When Canadian society is viewed in this light, we have paid a terrible price to avoid the Marxian prognostication. But with this knowledge, we now have a clearer idea of the fields in which tension must replace domination if the human condition is to be improved and fairness is to be restored to our economic system. That is, we can begin to reconstruct a new thought concreteness based on these new categories.

There is also another perspective from which one can view the failure of class consciousness to materialize. It needs to be recalled that Marx's fundamental quest is to solve the scarcity problem without alienation and injustice, and in his scenario this objective is accomplished in a world without a market economy and private property. In the process of achieving this state of affairs, it is necessary to co-opt disillusioned members of the capitalist class in order to maintain the technological apparatus. Any attempt to quicken the pace and precipitate revolutionary practice before this technological-managerial skill is supportive is destined to fail. Referring to early initiatives by St Simon, Fourier, and Owen to create socialist utopias, Marx stated, "The first great attempts of the proletariat to attain its own ends ... necessarily failed, owing to the then undeveloped state of the proletariat, as well as the absence of the economic conditions for its emancipation, conditions that were yet to be produced by the impending bourgeois epoch alone." (See Gouldner 1980, 195.) Successful revolution – in terms of both being accomplished and being able to generate consumption and investment goods after the new regime is in place – requires an advanced state of technology and a cadre of supporters with middle-class skills and expertise. In one sense, we are back to the same Skinnerian conclusion: the revolution failed because the middle class co-opted the proletariat rather than the opposite.

However, if we take this perspective and add a geographic dimension to it, the issue is altered. Now, instead of being a conflict among classes, it can be seen as a conflict among regions or nation states. If one chooses two countries in which one country dominates the other, say, the United States and Canada, the analogy becomes quite clear. Now, if it is assumed that some form of revolutionary praxis is initiated in Canada, then the technological apparatus can be sustained in the post-revolutionary period because the resources, the technology, and the skills are captured inside the net, merely because of location. In short, once a spatial dimension is added, the conditions necessary for sustaining revolutionary momentum are altered. (See Frank 1967.)

It is thus the ultimate in understatement to affirm that the dialectic analyst can learn an astonishing amount about methodology from Marx. His explanations of how, in the sweep of history, dialectic tensions become unbalanced and through friction are resolved to create a new social arrangement provide a paradigm for understanding the dynamics of underlying social processes. Studying his categories and errors leads to the discovery of other categories that are relevant to both universal and local knowledge in Canada.

But Marx is only one of many proponents of the dialectic, and the real excitement of this perspective stems from the fact that it allows one to co-ordinate the ideas of scholars with different philosophical, political, and religious persuasions under a single methodological umbrella.

6 The Policies

And thou America! I once beheld thee
but now behold no more.

If a dialectic analysis of the dimensions (totalities) comprising universal and local knowledge is undertaken within the context of the Canadian economy and if the analysis presupposes that it is in the public interest to establish tense dialectic relationships between the oppositional elements in each totality and if it is the responsibility of government to preserve the public interest, it is obvious that a new theoretical framework needs to be designed to guide policy. The general objective of the new system will be to eliminate domination rather than, as at present, to promote *the idea of progress* without reference to its dialectic consequences. More specifically, if one considers the following list of dimensions –

Technical reason	Imagination
Foreign control	Nationalism
Centre	Margin
Space	Time
Civilization	Nature
Men	Women
European	Native

it seems that current practices concentrate on the elements in the first column whereas the new disciplinary perspective would nurture those in the second column. It should be emphasized that this is not meant to be an exhaustive list of categories; additional dimensions can undoubtedly be revealed by further dialectic abstraction or by alternative methods of prefiguring.

It is instructive to note that while this perspective has humanistic roots, it shares common ground with both mainstream ideologies in the social sciences: Marxism and capitalism. For example, one of the main threads of critical Marxism, as articulated by the Frankfurt School, is that the domination of nature by technology inevitably leads to the domination of the citizenry and that this circumstance can only be eliminated by modifying the social arrangement. (See Jay 1973.) Furthermore, as our discussion unfolds it will become apparent that the new policy paradigm is also consistent with some ideas at the opposite end of the ideological spectrum, as expressed by Adam Smith in his *Wealth of Nations* and *Theory of Moral Sentiments*. Smith extolled the virtues of a society based on competition, the invisible hand, and sympathy, arguing that it was amenable to human growth and fulfilment. However, he did not anticipate that monopoly-dominated markets would become commonplace (as distinct from Marx, who anticipated that they would be commonplace but under-estimated their resilience). In order to approach the ideal state envis-aged by Smith, these monopoly elements need to be constrained; this is also a feature of the policy framework being developed.

In addition, the framework is relevant to the "end of history" debate that was recently in vogue. This controversy centres on the propo-sition that capitalism has won the war with socialism and is now firmly entrenched in the industrial world. However, one corollary to this line of reasoning is that the absence of an external threat to capitalist hegemony may make the system introspective, so that it begins to evaluate the numerous consequences of its own materialist orientation. To do so it needs to situate materialism in a cultural context and evaluate both its physical and metaphysical implications. However, there is a void in the orthodox evaluative arsenal, for as one analyst has observed, "the intellectual weight of [capitalist] mate-rialism is such that not a single respectable contemporary theory of economic development addresses consciousness and culture seriously as the matrix within which economic behavior is formed" (Fukuyama 1989). It is conceivable that our paradigm can help to fill this void.

The point of this brief preamble is that the new framework may appear to be idealistic but in fact it has linkages with authentic elements of mainstream social theories and, in addition, has rele-vance to issues of considerable contemporary concern. However, it would be naïve to underestimate the magnitude of change necessary to implement its imperatives. The institutional change would likely be on a scale equivalent to that currently being effected in Europe;

the attitudinal change would require that one see the existing system as a depressing exhibition of exploitation and fragmentation rather than a celebration of rationalism; the internal shift in the balance of power amongst interest groups would be similarly profound. However, if power is subject to the same conditions that Bentham observed about money – that it is subject to diminishing marginal utility except amongst the addicted and the perverse – and if mankind's freedom requires that the power possessed by adherents of the *idea of progress* be diminished, then change is preferable to the prospect of a society in which consumerism trivializes the human spirit and even threatens human existence.

In order to optimize the theory-praxis relationships within the new paradigm, it is prudent to make a judgment as to whether any particular dimension or totality should be given priority. In making this determination, one must be cognizant of the relative importance of each dimension but, in addition, seek to shape the theoretical framework in such a way that the possibility of implementing the necessary policy shifts is maximized.

One option is to proceed simultaneously on all fronts with equal vigour, building a balanced theory of economic development that elevates all the suppressed constituencies. However, it cannot go unnoticed that these groups have been relatively ineffective in the past, gaining only token recognition in the process of policy formation. Perhaps it is because they become single-issue interest groups who pick away at the edges of the well-financed and privileged *idea of progress* monolith but who individually lack sufficient support to force proponents of this orthodoxy to depart from their positivist evaluative and decision-making paradigms. If this observation is true, the lesson to be learned is that radical efforts must be co-ordinated and that there can only be an insurrection of subjugated knowledges if there is a coalition of those being subjugated. Fortunately, if the Atwood-Innis-Colville ideas about clustering have merit, the process can be natural rather than contrived.

Nevertheless, it would seem that to make a coalition effective a single dimension should be selected to act as a focus of initial action as well as a unifying symbol for what can eventually become a more broadly based reform. In selecting this dimension, nationalism becomes an obvious candidate because it is the only category that has a spatial aspect corresponding to a political jurisdiction. That is, if tense dialectic relationships are to be fostered across a wide range of totalities, there is a great advantage if a geographic area can first be secured within which the adverse features of the *idea of progress* can be constrained by legislation and policy. In other words, if we are to distance ourselves from the idea, we must also distance ourselves from its major protagonist, the United States, and seek to construct an alternative social arrangement built on our differences rather than our similarities.

ELEMENTS OF A DIALECTIC THEORY OF NATIONALISM

It is possible to describe some of the characteristics of the theoretical system that is envisaged.

• Its principle objective is to design policy proposals that reduce our dependence on the *idea of progress* and the United States while creating an environment in which tense dialectic relationships can be established between Canada's fundamental opposites.
• It should have a normative gestalt orientation and be formulated with recognition of the advantages and limitations that that entails. For example, as theory and policy formation blend together, there is a departure from the positivism and instrumentalism of orthodoxy. Nevertheless, many of the standard simulation and forecasting techniques of, say, econometrics will continue to be of use even though, in the short run, extrapolative procedures may be of limited value because the social ethos will be so different.
• It should design policies that assist in the transformation of society without having an adverse impact on the level of economic well-being of the nation. Among other things, this requirement involves the formulation of new criteria for the evaluation of technological and institutional systems.

While it is expeditious to concentrate initially on nationalism, this is only the prelude for a multidimensional program of change. In order to provide a preliminary overview of what is involved, it is instructive to indicate some of the implications of restructuring the nation according to the dictates of a gestalt dialectic criterion.

Let us first examine the rationality-imagination dimension and focus on the education of the nation's youth. For many teenagers these two poles have become unhinged and trivialized. Reasoning skills are underdeveloped: one-third of eighteen-year-olds are high-school dropouts, and many of those who remain are merely following what they believe to be the path of least resistance; understanding of humanistic and scientific concepts is rudimentary; knowledge of national and global communities and of the interactions between social institutions is meagre. At the opposite pole, imaginative skills are similarly retarded: the primary occupation of many is to watch and listen to the performances of others and to obtain vicarious enjoyment through often pathetic emulation; curiosity is channelled into activities that offer instant gratification; fantasies become frivolous and narcissistic. In short, we are nurturing an immense subculture of teenagers whose learning abilities are being stifled by the unhinging of reason and imagination and who, as adults, will be doubly stressed because of the disjunction between their abilities and their modernist expectations. In the search for the cause of this malaise one can refer to the various issues outlined in chapter two. In the search for solutions, the focus should be to establish interpenetration between reason and imagination in the minds of our young citizens and to engender an understanding that the benefits of symbiosis rise exponentially. Economists can participate in this search by examining, for example, the feasibility of behaviourist control mechanisms and censorship and the practicality of institutional changes such as curriculum redesign and the expansion of second-chance safety nets. The traditional measurement tools of the economist will be invaluable in this endeavour, but the theory itself will have to emanate from disciplines currently outside the economics umbrella. Frye (1990) provides a framework with assimilative potential. He identifies four interpenetrating modes of expression in literature: descriptive, conceptual, rhetorical, and imaginative. Orthodox economists are comfortable with the first two modes, flirt nervously with the third (McCloskey 1983), and ignore the fourth. To do so is to threaten the welfare of the nation, for if the above assessment of teenagers is correct, the subjugation, isolation, and trivialization of their imaginations can have enormous economic costs arising from lost productivity, maldistribution of income, expanded social services, and so on. If rationality is a legitimate economic concept, so also is imagination. The two must be integrated in the pursuit of an improved understanding of existing cogent ideas and, through transcendence, in the discovery of new ones. The theoretical and practical challenges are both formidable and one must not underestimate the difficulty of methodological metamorphosis and of, say, replacing Madonna as a role model. However, one must also be cognizant of the enormous costs of not doing so.

Another dimension in which nationalism will permit one to reveal and to rectify chronic imperfections imposed by orthodoxy and the *idea of progress* is that which links spatial and temporal considerations. Atwood and Innis have described the overwhelming domination of spatial exploitation in shaping both our historical development and our collective conscience. Our desecrated natural environments provide visible evidence of the myopia involved in these processes, as does our enormous fiscal deficit. In the latter case, while it is true that the long-run consequences of the debt depend on the nature of the expenditures which are made possible and on the manner in which it is financed, future generations are invariably left with an unfavourable legacy comprised of a repayment burden and a maldistribution of income. Economists have a variety of tools that can be used to elevate the significance of temporal considerations in policy making. For example, they are knowledgeable about time preference functions, debt reduction procedures, and the measurement of externalities associated with industrial processes. However, as in the case of the linkage of rationality and imagination, a comprehensive theory of this dimension is more likely to emanate from other disciplines. Two potential candidates come to mind: environmentalism and post-modern literature.

At present, the most mature understanding of relevant temporal issues is probably contained in the subset of environmental literature that uses the entropy law as its core theoretical concept. (See Rifkin 1980.) Furthermore, the environmental movement may be a useful model for the actualization of our own program, because it has led to a reasonable effective coalition between the scientific community and humanists. The former, perceiving the economic system as a process whose fundamental activities relate to the transformation, consumption, and excretion of energy, demonstrate that survival is contingent on our ability to switch from non-renewable to renewable sources; the latter provide the moral underpinning for the social change that is required. (See Daly 1980.) Perhaps surprisingly, there is a companion philosophy expressed in those post-modern literary works that emphasize the inevitability of decay and the ironies of technological innovation. (See Pynchon 1973.) The task is to adapt an entropy-based theoretical framework to the analysis of economic issues such as resource pricing and intergenerational equity. In so doing, economists will shift their focus from the current preoccupation with the present and also become guardians of the rights of the unborn.

Another important dimension is the one bounded by the centre and margin poles, a conceptualization that can be used to describe a wide area of geographic, political, ethnic, demographic, and gender-related phenomena. Historically, the geographic manifestation of this oppositional has been among the more compelling determinants of the rhythms and perturbations of Canada's evolution. For this reason, orthodox economics has generated a vast theoretical literature rooted in geography – location, dependency, and trade theories, for example – and combined it with theories of industrial structure to try to explain the nation's character. These theories are reflected in regional development policies and in a variety of other decisions which have spatial implications.

One should be cautions about proffering blanket condemnations, but if one uses, say, provincial per capita income statistics as an indicator, it is safe to conclude that past policies have not solved the problems in the hinterlands and there is a continuing need to address them. The search for the best method of doing so has led to controversy between liberals and conservatives, although cynics might point to increasing evidence that public decisions that influence industrial location are more often based on the geographic distribution of political power than on ideological considerations. Shifting to a dialectic perspective provides a consistent, politically neutral set of objectives. There is no guarantee that they can be achieved. However, recent crises in the fishing, forestry, and agriculture industries suggest that some change in direction is imperative. Often change itself creates opportunities. A recent book about Alberta (Mansell and Percy, 1989) discusses the mechanics and potentialities of sharp policy shifts to counteract economic stagnation, in this case, diversification because of sluggishness in the energy sector. The title, *Strength through Adversity*, summarizes its main thesis: adversity can be a blessing in disguise if it engenders new perspectives and the search for new opportunities. That necessity can sometimes be the mother of invention is a universal truth which is applicable across all the dimensions of our paradigm.

It any case, the orthodox treatment of the centre-margin issue needs to be modified in at least two ways to make it consistent with the new perspective. First, issues should be conceptualized as manifestations of fundamental opposites with the objective of fostering sustainable tension rather than encouraging unhinging and domination. This would preclude, for example, many current federal policies which are shifting economic power to the marketplace, an institutional arrangement that has notorious centrist tendencies, both structural and locational.

Second, centre-margin thought patterns should be extended to areas outside the domain of orthodox economics. Aboriginal rights and gender equality are logical candidates. In the former case, recent decisions by the federal government with respect to land claims and native self-government suggest that tension and transcendence are already seen as the appropriate path to reform, although it is difficult to determine whether these initiatives are motivated by an ideological shift or are an *ad hoc* response to guilt and pressure. In the case of gender equality, the record is less promising. Recent data concerning circumstances in the workplace suggest the domination continues to be the rule rather than the exception.

Aspects of the centre-margin issue are also present in the complex dialectic relationship between English and French Canada, which has occupied the nation's attention in recent years. The tone of this dialectic was set in 1774 when Quebec was granted the right to preserve its religion, seigneurial system, and civil legal code and in subsequent years by legislation that protected the French language. Two centuries later, if one listens to separatists, unhinging rather than transcendence is seen as a solution. Given the current state of flux and the difficulty of separating posturing from commitment, it is not possible to predict the outcome of this controversy with any degree of confidence. However, if the issue is cast within our dialectic framework, certain conclusions become obvious. First, the relationship must be flexible enough to accommodate a shifting configuration of tensions. This conclusion is understood by Simeon, who made the following statement in an article discussing the 1982 Constitution and the Meech Lake Accord:

Tensions, ambiguities and contradictions are built into both documents, whether taken individually or together. This should not be surprising; the balancing between region and nation, provinces and the federal government, French and English has been the central characteristic of Canadian politics and of its constitutional documents throughout its history. No one model has been able to predominate. We must continually balance and redefine competing viewpoints. To impose one and exclude others is a recipe for fundamental conflict. The question for Meech Lake, then, is whether it gets the balance right, and whether under it, Canada retains the ability to shift the balance in response to changed attitudes and circumstances. (Simeon 1988, S23)

The fact that the Meech Lake Accord did not get the balance right does not negate the basic premise. Second, the issue can be characterized as a fundamental opposite, with the primary dialectic between French Quebec and English Canada bound together by such forces as bilingualism, numerous shared attitudes, a high regard for each other, and the realization that economic union is mutually beneficial. The primary tension is reinforced by secondary dialectic links connecting linguistic minorities to the larger population in each region. These secondary links are reinforcing because they encourage civility, cordiality, and tolerance. Given this conceptualization and the arguments presented in previous chapters, certain conclusions become obvious. Distinct societies are to be encouraged but transcended; the fundamental mandate of governments is to erode domination; the expenses of binding, if reasonable, are a benefit rather than a cost; cultural interpenetration is to be encouraged to bring regional variations in local knowledge into sharper focus. This simple statement of principles abstracts from the complexity of nuance and ignores the difficulty of implementation, but the objective is unambiguous.

The line of reasoning just presented can be summarized as follows. The dialectic framework needs to be extended beyond its nationalist plane into multidimensional space. Indeed, nationalism is a mere precondition. In the construction of a multidimensional gestalt paradigm and the implementation of its imperatives, one will be required to draw on the theories and practices of several intellectual disciplines. In some dimensions, the theoretical core will originate outside economics so that concepts such as imagination and entropy are brought into the analytical domain. In others, the intellectual flow will be reversed as mainstream economic theories are applied to a wider array of phenomena. For example, as "maximization subject to constraint" models are transformed into a gestalt system, some constraints become intrinsic penetrators. While each dimension of the system has its own unique features, they share a common theme, tension, and because of clustering, an internally consistent paradigm can be constructed.

However, articulation is easier than actualization, and before we become too enthusiastic about the potentialities of a complex multidimensional framework, it is prudent to pause and inquire about the likelihood that it can be implemented. This depends primarily on the feasibility of creating a nationalistic environment of the type envisaged. About this issue two related questions need to be answered: at the conceptual level is it desirable, and if so, can it be achieved without undue economic cost? These questions will be addressed serially.

What is deemed to be desirable needs to reflect the will of the people. Historically Canadians have experienced "viceral spasms" of nationalist sentiment at periods separated by stretches of resignation to continentalist pressures and attractions. Recent events demonstrating the global power of conservatism suggest that the latter attitude is on the ascendency. However, it is my belief that the apparent impotence of nationalism is a result of perceiving reality through the lens of the *idea of progress* and that this is an *alien paradigm* that leads to perceptions which thwart resolve. Several examples can be identified: political will is dissipated by intellectual fragmentation;

conservative rhetoric takes on the illusion of plausibility; nationalism is identified as a ploy to serve the interests of the unproductive; the American way of life is emulated; the adverse consequences of market forces are tolerated; regional and local loyalties are substituted for nationalism; Canadian institutions are patterned after those at the centre of empire. Each of these perceptions, which will be described briefly, can be shown to be misguided when evaluated with reference to the proposed dialectic paradigm.

The question of fragmentation is discussed by Rotstein (1978), who notes that historically we tended to view nationalism solely as a spatial phenomena "confined to a single dimension of political concern: the integrity of Canadian territory from sea to sea, and the integrity of legal jurisdiction and social order on that territory." When analysis is undertaken with such a narrow objective and within the confines of traditional disciplinary boundaries, unifying threads are weak or absent. A gestalt methodology unites different perspectives into a program of action that can engender an effective coalition of previously fragmented interest groups.

Nationalist will has also been dissipated, particularly in the 1980s, by the popularity of conservative rhetoric. For example, if the continentalist issue is approached from within the framework of orthodox economics, one is led inexorably to the conclusion that spatial hierarchies are desirable and it is natural that Canada be subservient to the United States. That is, wealth and activity should gravitate to the populated heartlands to take advantage of scale and agglomeration economies. This is not the conclusion of an indigenous dialectic model that tracks the forces within the Canadian society and seeks to counteract exploitation.

Another argument often used to discredit Canadian nationalism is the claim that it is a thinly disguised subterfuge designed to insulate a parochial privileged class. This position is advanced forcefully by Breton (1964), who believes that advocates of tariffs are merely trying to expand the income of the entrenched local labouring, managerial, and capitalist classes. His argument crumbles when confronted by the new paradigm whose nationalism has egalitarian rather than élitist roots.

However, perhaps the most forceful impact of the *idea of progress* on Canadian attitudes and behaviour is that it conditions us to emulate, rather than resist, the American way. History abounds with examples of colonized nations who willingly sacrifice their cultural distinctiveness in order to ingratiate themselves to the apparently more sophisticated overseers. In the Canadian case, we had a distinctive origin. "The very foundation of Canada was to be something different from the United States, was to build a society that was more ordered, that was more reasonable, that wasn't so full of illusions, that wasn't so full of violence, that wasn't so full of dreams as the Americans" (Grant 1986, 2). However, over time we drifted willingly toward hegemony, conquered by our own desire rather than their demands, succumbing into acquiescent compliance. Many commentators have described this process, but an explanation by Crean and Rioux (1982) is particularly useful. They analyse cultural penetrations in North America and distinguish between high culture, mass culture, and popular culture. The first is dedicated to the pursuit of understanding about the complexities of human existence. The second involves the design of mentations to escape from these complexities. The third is participatory and seeks to develop individual character through praxis. America is said to maintain its empire by exporting mass culture, and even the harshest critics are in awe of its ability to market escapism so effectively that it becomes an elemental instrument of imperialism.

Canadians can expect this subservience to persist as long as we continue to function within the aegis of the *idea of progress*. However, if a dialectic nationalism is created, the impact of American cultural penetration is inverted to become a force that fortifies rather than erodes independence. That is, America can still be expected to export its culture, but when this culture is examined in the context of the new paradigm, it is seen to be a fiction and its underlying social arrangement to be grossly defective. If this perspective is adopted, what is now entertainment becomes educational, so that *mass culture turns into high culture* and what used to be a gravitational attraction reverses its force field. The same artifacts and influences that now threaten our integrity become positive contributors to the process of personal emancipation and antecedents on the path leading toward the kind of transcendence conceptualized earlier as universal knowledge. A shift in the method used to evaluate phenomena takes a force that now generates subservience and transposes it to become a source of enlightenment.

Another reason why Canadians seem to be reluctant to embrace nationalism is that we are said to possess a habit of mind which prefers tolerance, compromise, and accommodation rather than the high degree of assertiveness that is necessary to achieve independence. This tolerance was probably imprinted on us during our early history when it was necessary to accommodate both the French and English, but it has been reinforced by the subsequent flow of events. For example, settlement did not produce untoward conflict: in the homesteading era, spaciousness allowed new immigrants to settle without unduly threatening the customs of established communities; during urbanization, rapid economic growth permitted the assimilation of waves of immigrants with a minimum of ethnic or employment-related discord. This underlying tolerance was reinforced by our evolving institutional arrangements. Justice embedded in the rule of law became the only acceptable method of resolving disputes, and as Woodcock and Simeon pointed out earlier, our legislative history is marked by the need to balance competing interests. Because of these types of forces we emerged as an ungainly, hesitant adolescent, reacting and responding rather than initiating and asserting. This passiveness is undoubtedly reinforced by our role in the international community. We are a relatively unimportant player in the world of military alliances, interlocking technologies, multinational corporations, and financial conglomerates, and consequently a stance of tolerant quietude seems appropriate.

Once again we have fallen into the trap of evaluating ourselves within an alien paradigm. In an *idea of progress* world our record of achievements does not justify anything other than passive inaction and compliant followership. The tolerance arising from our historical experiences meshes with the mediocrity of our international stature to make stoicism seem to be a natural, and even a noumenal, attribute. However, if our situation is conceptualized within the new framework, tolerance becomes a basis of action designed to ensure that tense dialectic relationships are established and maintained. For example, to be tolerant of women's values requires that they be given an opportunity to be fulfilled. Similarly, to be tolerant of popular culture requires that it be free to exercise its imperatives without being oppressed by an imported mass culture. The new paradigm allows us to invert the concept of tolerance so that we not only exhibit it, we demand it for the oppressed polarities of our fundamental opposites.

Another factor that impedes the formation of a resolute nationalistic consciousness is that in many cases our primary loyalty is to the local region. (See Frye 1971.) Such loyalty is understandable. Man's sensitivities are egocentric, emanating outward from the self to the family, the neighbourhood, the community, and so on. Furthermore, the immediate can be more easily comprehended because one can employ the full array of senses, reason, and the imagination whereas more distant and abstract concepts such as the nation are elusive. The regionalism arising from these psychological limitations is reinforced by an array of societal realities. Our mosaic heritage means that popular ethnic culture can be related directly to universal knowledge, making it appear that the nation is not a relevant category in matters dealing with cultural expression. The heterogeneity of our resource base and topography invites locational specialization. Provincial political leaders are typically strident and parochial. The city rather than the nation has become the dominant community in society, for it is within the urban agglomeration that the essential production and distribution networks are established, perceptions are imprinted, class distinctions are articulated, and allegiances are formed. (See Jacobs 1984.) As a consequence, many Canadians feel that the nation is redundant because values are shaped in the crucible of forces from American metropolises and sensations derived from stimuli in the immediate environment. Nationalism is squeezed by both imperialism and regionalism: the fruits of the *idea of progress* are identified with the ethos of the former and made available by the bounty of the latter.

However, regionalism is inverted in a dialectic paradigm. When the function of the central government is to dampen the ubiquity of the *idea of progress*, regionalism and nationalism become symbiotic. That is, if the role of the central government is to deflect the penetration of external forces, provincial governments are encouraged to direct their attention to the fulfilment of authentic regional aspirations and the creation of tense interregional dialectic relationships. In such an atmosphere, federal-provincial relationships cease to be a simple division of power within the format of a zero-sum game, for an expansion of federal power to preclude exploitive practices by non-nationals enhances the ability of provincial governments to choose their own development patterns. In turn, diverse regional interests generate tensions that make the Canadian social fabric more resilient. Thus, within a dialectic framework, regionalism is no longer a barrier to nationalism but instead is inverted to become a symbiotic partner.

The final obstacle to nationalism to be mentioned is our willingness to accept local replicas of the symbols and institutions of the nations that have colonized our land and our minds. Rotstein refers to this as derivative liberalism.

The greatest weakness in the set of requirements for preserving Canadian independence is the peculiar intellectual and political tradition that forms the present basis of the Canadian political culture. In brief, we are the legatees of a transplanted political tradition stemming from classical English liberalism. While we have gained the legal trappings of sovereignty and independence, we are unable to muster the symbols and the political vocabulary necessary to understand the vital interests of this country and to act for its preservation. The essential weakness of the Canadian political culture lies in its derivative liberalism. This is the heritage of an intellectual colonialism, concepts and symbols of which are inadequate to our dilemma and bypass the major problems surrounding Canadian independence. (Rotstein 1973, 191)

In more recent years this influence has eroded somewhat, largely because of assertiveness by those seeking recognition as distinct societies within the Canadian cultural matrix. Nevertheless, the dependence persists and will continue to do so for as long as the *idea of progress* is supreme. However, it can be broken if decisions concerning symbols and institutions are made with reference to criteria established within an indigenous dialectic model. Under such circumstances, derivative liberalism can be inverted to become the kind of conservatism favoured by Grant.

Thus it is seen that many of the barriers to nationalism are the result of viewing reality through the lens of the *idea of progress*. If the lens is changed so as to be consistent with the dialectic realities of the Canadian system, these impediments evaporate. Political will is no longer dissipated by a fragmented analytical structure; conservative rhetoric loses its seductiveness; egalitarian interests are no longer confused with élitism; the artifacts and influences that are now the basis of emulation become antecedents to transcendence as mass culture is transformed into high culture; tolerance is converted into an assertive demand to be tolerated; regionalism and nationalism become symbiotic as the predatory practices of non-nationals are precluded; derivative liberalism is the embryo from which Grant's conservatism evolves. While one must not underestimate the struggle involved in implementing a nationalistic agenda, a case can be made that it is possible, logical, and in the interests of human fulfilment, necessary. In short, it is desirable.

However, nationalism must not only be desirable, it must be feasible. That is, the transition must be achieved without undue economic cost. Conventional orthodox wisdom – based on Ricardian models, but ignoring the theory of second best – suggests that such a transition is not possible and that nationalistic policies will have adverse impacts on economic performance. This view is predicated upon three major considerations: belief that the policies cause inefficiencies and distortions; fear associated with the loss of access to American markets and sources of capital; concern that isolation is counterproductive, particularly since the dynamics of international trade exhibits a trend toward the establishment of large trading blocks. As we shall see in a moment, nationalists can counter each of these arguments with plausible rebuttals. However, it should be noted at the outset that in spite of the rhetoric emanating from both opponents and proponents, the economic consequences of any future shift toward nationalism are unknown. The uncertainty arises because we cannot anticipate all future behaviour patterns and because there are limits to the relevance of past experience, primarily because there is an asymmetry in the course of events. That is, Canada has taken a century to arrive at its present state of foreign domination, and a nationalistic reversal does not return us to a pristine state but rather to something we have not yet experienced. Mantling and dismantling foreign control is not the same as getting dressed and then undressed. The following discussion should be interpreted within the context of these limitations.

The continentalist's claims that nationalism causes inefficiencies and distortions is one of the sacred cows of orthodoxy. It is based primarily on the notion that nationalism limits the opportunities for scale economies and reduces access to foreign technology, capital, and markets. A case can be made for these claims in the pristine world of orthodox undergraduate textbooks, but this world is far removed from contemporary Canada, where the existing arrangement is already laden with distortions such as monopoly and foreign control. As Watkins (1978) indicates, this is a policy-induced phenomenon resulting from a century of misdirected initiatives. Sometimes these initiatives were undertaken in the interests of protectionism; sometimes to stimulate expansion without specific reference to ownership and location of markets. The most common characteristic was probably myopia: governments are attracted to visible, capital-intensive projects because of the positive economic spin-offs during the initial construction period, and they unwittingly nourish activities that face problems or cause adverse externalities during their production phases. When nationalistic policies are introduced into such a morass, they need not be counter to the public interest! To take a simple illustration: it is possible that the advantages associated with, say, curtailing the monopolistic practices of foreign multinationals are greater than the losses arising from reduced opportunities for scale economies, particularly if the definition of the "public interest" is negotiable.

One dimension of existing distortion that should be of special concern to Canadians is the exploitation of natural resources where fragile ecological systems are affected. Here development occurs with reference to both profitability and regulatory policy. Both have been profoundly myopic, the private sector because of the practice of using discount rates related to business risk rather than intergenerational equity (Georgescu-Roegen 1971) and the public regulators because, as Stigler noted years ago, they are conditioned to protect producers rather than consumers. As an aside, it is worth noting that orthodox economics has constructed a sophisticated tool, the Hotelling rule, to allay fears about premature resource depletion. However, this is only an elaborate subterfuge because, contrary to the thrust of the rhetoric, the rule is an equilibrium condition in a perfectly competitive market and not an effective safety net for a small, open economy riddled with market imperfections. The truth of the matter is that in the present global environment, the lowest cost and most secure resources are exploited first and nations such as Canada that possess these resources are vulnerable to premature exploitation.

This line of reasoning emphasizes the irony of historical events because policies invariably have long-run consequences that are opposite to short-run intentions. We have seen previously that the National Policy, while designed to make us independent, has made us dependent. Now we see that the pursuit of economic growth has led to an economy laden with distortions in which the government is held hostage by a monopolistic, foreign controlled, and myopic private sector. This realization provides two insights that can aid in the design of an effective nationalistic theory and related policies. For one thing, it destroys the *idea of progress* myth that nationalism involves the imposition of restrictions on an otherwise competitive market system. In reality, it introduces a non-market element into a distorted market system, and its effectiveness, even using orthodox criteria, depends on the extent to which it assists in the elimination of these distortions. In addition, by emphasizing the temporal profile of economic benefits and costs and the possibility of premature resource exploitation, it demonstrates that nationalism may be the most effective way of establishing a more satisfactory distribution of well-being between present and future generations. This outcome is surely in the public interest, however defined.

The second continentalist claim relates to the idea that nationalism will destroy our relationship with the United States. The validity of this argument hinges, of course, on the way that the nationalist thrust is actualized. Let us presuppose that the initial operational objective is to balance our current account and that a policy mix including tariffs, non-tariff barriers, exchange rate variations, a revised competition policy, and possibly a modified taxation regime is introduced to accomplish this. Is this a feasible program?

Canada's current account dilemma is well known. In most years we have a trade surplus that is overbalanced by net outflows of service payments – principally for interest and dividends on past foreign investment – to create a current account deficit. This state of affairs necessitates further capital inflows, exacerbating the deficit problem in future years. (Historically most of the foreign capital has originated in the United States. However, in recent years offshore investors have become increasingly active.) The problem intensifies to the point that fiscal and monetary policy have to be deflected from the pursuit of domestic objectives and designed to continually attract foreign capital! It becomes a sad irony that our policy levers are now used to make us increasingly subservient.

It is hard to imagine that any fair-minded individual would object to a Canadian decision to seek to balance its current account. Unquestionably there are special interest groups who will not be in favour, but to seek a "balance" is a perfectly legitimate national objective. This is particularly true if the mechanisms used to accomplish it are consistent with practices employed elsewhere in the industrial world.

One mechanism that already has considerable public support is to lower exchange rates, thereby altering the configuration of prices for both exports and imports. This policy might be accompanied by lower interest rates, which in turn can encourage domestic investment during the period when the economy adjusts to a nationalist agenda. There is also a tactical advantage to the use of exchange rates as a policy lever because unlike trade barriers, it is not something that can be negated by retaliatory American policy. If one recalls recent events, it will be remembered that in the early 1980s Americans first vacuumed up massive amounts of foreign capital to finance their own domestic growth and then, encountering trade deficits, devalued their currency. The United States can scarcely object if Canada embarks on a similar course of action in the 1990s. Nor are Americans in a position to lower their rates correspondingly, because they must be kept attuned to the rates of their more powerful trading partners in Western Europe and Asia.

It should not be inferred that the lowering of exchange rates is a panacea because there would undoubtedly be some unfavourable price movements. However, it is an appropriate candidate for inclusion in a policy package. The rate is managed at present; all that is being suggested is that it be managed according to a new criterion.

A second mechanism is selective tariff protection even though it can lead to retaliation and engender costly activities associated with import substitution. Any new system needs to be designed with reference to these considerations and the legal commitments we have with our trading partners. However, there is also a more fundamental issue that relates to the inconsistency between true efficiency and the vulgar use of the term, in which it is equated with profitability. The case for nationalism rests on the former because it provides a basis for expanding the range of choices available to the citizenry; the case for continentalism too often relates to the latter interpretation. With reference to, say, the Free Trade Agreement, one must ask who really benefits from trade liberalization in a world characterized by materialism, commercial control of the media, skyrocketing debt, planned obsolescence, and energy-intensive technologies. One suspects that it is someone other than the citizen who is searching for a more enlightened and fulfilling lifestyle. If our line of reasoning is correct, he will benefit, not from a dismantling of tariffs, but rather from a refocusing that heightens tensions between the nation's fundamental opposites.

A similar refocusing is possible amongst non-tariff barriers, a weapon that has proven to be a potent method of achieving national objectives. For example, the skill with which the Japanese use linguistic and administrative obstacles to discourage imports is well documented; furthermore, the use of quotas and subsidies has become an art form practised with masterful skill, particularly by Europeans. The ubiquity of these practices is illustrated by the following headlines in a single newspaper, which is selected solely because it arrived on the day that this section was first being drafted:

The President signed into law a $4 bn rescue bill for the troubled U.S. farm credit system.

The European Community said it was giving about $120 m to fishermen of member states to help them improve their fleets.

U.S. is seeking formal talks with the European Community over a complaint from the American Soybean Association which claims increasing European subsidies have caused U.S. soybean exports to Europe to drop to about $2 bn a year from $3.7 bn five years ago.

The U.S. refused a Japanese request to remove import sanctions imposed for alleged violations of the U.S.-Japan semi-conductor trade pact.

Caribbean sugar exporters who have been struggling to keep their industries alive have been angered by the latest cuts of 25% in import quotas by the U.S.

A similar array of reports can be found on any day in any business paper, because the fact of the matter is that over half of the world's trade is conducted under terms that defy General Agreement of Tariffs and Trade (GATT) rules. In reality, the scope for non-tariff barriers is immense. Furthermore, judging from the performance of countries who use them skilfully, they do not represent the threat to national economic viability that one might infer from reading the conclusions of orthodox textbooks; rather they are an effective means of achieving national objectives. There is no reason why they too cannot be designed to nurture and sustain tension between Canada's fundamental opposites.

Another element in a nationalist economic program must be a vigorous policy to enhance competitive conditions in Canada without undue bureaucratization of the regulatory mechanism. In doing so, a series of enormously difficult questions about the nature of competition must be addressed: the relationship between firm size and efficiency and between structure and performance; the viability of a key industry strategy; the modalities of successful innovation; and so on. These questions have heretofore defied unambiguous answers, although we are continuously bombarded with proposals. For example, a recent report (Porter 1991) suggests that in order to improve our competitive position we must upgrade our workforce, encourage technological innovation particularly in industries that have an underlying comparative advantage, intensify domestic rivalry, foster locational clustering, construct cost-effective infrastructure, reduce interprovincial trade barriers, and encourage attitudinal shifts amongst factor owners and consumers. Many of these proposals are no more difficult to implement in a nationalist environment than they are under continentalism. It may even be easier! That is, the plate of competitive restructuring will inevitably be full, and it may be made more palatable by controlling some variables in the interests of nationalism. Perhaps surprisingly, this process will not require major parliamentary initiative because enabling legislation is already in place and policy is shaped by interpretation. For example, the Competition Act and the Investment Canada Act give the federal government control over mergers and foreign investment. The present administration has operationalized its economic philosophy by taking a very permissive stance. An alternative perspective could be similarly operationalized by redefining what is meant by cases in which a merger "substantially lessens competition" or foreign investment is of "net benefit to Canada."

The use of these traditional tools – exchange rate variations, protectionism, and an active competition policy – can potentially lead to a balanced current account. It will be difficult for our trading partners to object because they have all employed similar means to satisfy their own national objectives when it has suited their purposes. It is now a Canadian purpose that is relevant. As a corollary, it should be noted that there are also more aggressive and controversial means of achieving balance. For example, one can introduce a policy in which a corporation's effective tax rate depends on the degree to which it is foreign owned. To the extent that such a policy encourages foreign firms to sell out to Canadian interests, it is also likely to decrease the degree of monopoly in our industrial structure. Undoubtedly, there will be charges that a tiered tax system which discriminates against foreign ownership is unjust. However, as Macpherson (1985) has pointed out, justice is a concept that is time and space specific because it must be defined with reference to a given set of social arrangements. In a society committed to property rights, we discriminate against those who steal; in a society committed to the *idea of progress*, we discriminate against those who cannot cope with the rigours of the market-place; in a society committed to dialectic nationalism, we will discriminate against forces such as foreign ownership that dominate and that propagate the *idea of progress*. In reality, a discriminatory tax regime can contribute to both distributive justice (i.e., related to the allocation of income and opportunity) and commutative justice (i.e., related to the assurance that different segments of society cannot be exploited by weak bargaining positions).

The third continentalist argument is that nationalism will isolate Canada from the world's large trading blocks. However, this is not necessarily true. Indeed, nationalism is consistent with bargained multilateralism, particularly if balanced interregional current accounts are accepted as operational guidelines. Ideally, Canadian exports would be patterned with reference to our resource base, skills, and innovative accomplishments, and our level of imports conditioned by our own successes. Reciprocity also cushions one against shocks and increases the degree of flexibility in adapting to changing circumstances. In this latter regard, it is interesting to note the recent prognostications of Toffler (1990). He argues that the world is embarking on a radical new system of wealth creation featuring computer-driven technologies and information-intensive goods and services. This shift will make both orthodox economic theory and mass production techniques increasingly obsolete. In future, success will require new conceptual categories focused on activities which are locationally footloose but which "turn out small runs of increasingly customized outputs aimed at niche markets." If these conditions materialize, one can anticipate a period of international flux and this might be a propitious time to undertake a complementary nationalistic restructuring. If Canada can be on the cutting edge of a new world trading order rather than, as historically, fulfilling the laggard's role as a supplier of raw materials for initiatives taken elsewhere, the result may be international conjunction and leadership rather than isolation and subservience.

The timeliness of nationalism is reinforced by the fact that Canada may be in the midst of a dramatic dialectic inversion in attitudes. In 1988 the conservative government approved the continentalist Free Trade Agreement. The long-run consequences of this initiative are difficult to predict because one does not know how events would have otherwise unfolded. In any case, its continuation is probably more dependent on perception than on actuality and on the manner in which this perception is reflected in voting behaviour. On one hand, there is a plausible scenario in which a conservative government retains power and proceeds with its agenda. However, at the time of writing the government seems vulnerable, perhaps because it has governed badly but perhaps also because its orthodox responses have not ameliorated problems arising from an array of destabilizing perturbations: a recession, industrial relocation, a new and unpopular taxation regime, the emergence of strident regional political parties, systemic failures in the cultural apparatus, financial strains within our helping agencies, and shocks in export markets associated with GATT inadequacies, countervailing duty disputes, realignment of power blocks, and war. If this government is defeated, it is not inconceivable that its successor will reject continentalism.

Should such a change occur, there will have been an inversion because the free trade initiative will have helped to precipitate a flow of events culminating in a resurgence of nationalistic sentiments. It is a possibility that reflects both the ironic capriciousness of events and the credibility of Hegelian methodology. However, if a new government is to be effective, it must nurture these sentiments so that they coalesce into a viable force. To assist this process it is desirable to have a theoretical system already in place to guide the energy into productive activities rather than have it degenerate into a useless chorus of whining invectives about the evils of continentalism. Elaboration of this theory and the formulation of a specific program in which nationalism might be achieved without undue economic sacrifice should become a primary task of Canada's academic economists.

Hence it is concluded that nationalism is desirable, feasible, and timely. But if nationalism is the game, the real prize is the possibility of achieving a more enlightened social arrangement based on a coalition of universal and local knowledge in which we seek to establish tense dialectic relationships between an array of fundamental opposites.

7 A Summary

Many a promising life has been spoiled by a happy childhood.

Orthodox economics is an intellectual discipline that analyses the way in which human beings produce, distribute, and consume goods in a market economy. It is also a major component in the superstructure that supports the *idea of progress*, the world-view which has dominated Western society for more than two centuries.

Orthodoxy has achieved high status by adopting a scientific perspective when explaining economic phenomena. It uses pure, rather than gestalt, theory and defines the boundaries of its domain by a specific set of generic axioms, including the proposition that man is innately materialistic. The origin of this axiom can be traced back to the discipline's founder, Adam Smith. He recognized that human beings have a materialistic tendency but felt that it would be constrained by compassion and competition and be directed toward noble ends by the desire for refinement. However, such a conceptualization is not amenable to scientific analysis, so Smith's followers discarded it and replaced it with a narrower interpretation of the human condition, which became crystallized as *economic man*. As orthodox economics evolved through its classical, neo-classical, and Keynesian phases, this interpretation has become more and more entrenched.

One of the deficiencies of the orthodox perspective is that it fails to recognize the existence of intentional deterministic (phenomenal) forces in the economic system. These forces are becoming increasingly significant in the real world as technology becomes more sophisticated. It follows that *economic man* has become a consequence as well as a cause of the *idea of progress*. Furthermore, he is shown to be normatively inferior, primarily because his range of freedoms is limited by this same technology.

This deficiency places orthodoxy in a dilemma because, though committed to the pursuit of the optimal, it supports a social arrangement that is generating a sub-optimal output, *economic man*. One solution is to reform the discipline so that its objective becomes the creation of a more normatively satisfactory state of human existence and technology and social organization become the means by which this is accomplished.

The process of disciplinary reform is an arduous undertaking because orthodoxy is supported by an elaborate network of interest groups who historically have demonstrated great resolve in protecting themselves when their positions of power are threatened by the prospect of change. However, Michel Foucault has investigated the anatomy of these networks and concluded that disciplines such as economics have a soft underbelly that makes them vulnerable. Specifically, they are guilty of a subterfuge in which truth is distorted to become disciplinary knowledge, which in turn is transposed into conventional wisdom and becomes a guideline for human action. In the process, truth is disconnected from action, so that the intellectual integrity of the discipline becomes suspect and open to criticism. This argument supports the conclusions of my own assessment, but more importantly Foucault also outlines a strategy for overcoming this predicament. He points out that when the significance of disciplinary knowledge is elevated, two other dimensions of knowledge, the universal and the local, are suppressed, not because they lack integrity but because they lack the appropriate degree of scientism. Reform requires a coalition of these dimensions in an "insurrection of subjugated knowledges." This implies that the normatively satisfying state of human existence which is the objective of a reformed discipline should include elements of both universal and local knowledge.

Universal knowledge can be defined as the underlying principles that give meaning to existence. The core theme in this constellation is the myth of deliverance, as presented in the Bible and adapted to contemporary circumstances in Western literature. In the context of my own purpose, it seems reasonable to concentrate on authors whose primary concern is deliverance from the *idea of progress*. William Blake, Søren Kierkegaard, and Paul Tillich are representatives of this school of thought.

Blake wrote during the early phases of the industrial revolution and was repelled by the rationalism and banal materialism it embodied. His art and poetry present an interpretation of human history which explains that mankind has reached this sorry state by allowing his world to be fragmented (i.e., man separated from woman, body separated from soul, man separated from God) and his reason to dominate his other energies (i.e., passion, sensation, and instinct). To escape from this morass, man must resituate the divine within himself and through use of his imagination, reassemble his fragmented parts into a unity.

Blake's work provides insights as to how universal knowledge can be structured. Specifically, he suggests that transcendence (i.e., deliverance) requires that the relationship between imagination and reason be symbiotic and though they are contraries, be held together as a unity, devoid of domination. He also explains the dynamics of transcendence and applies his theory to everyday economic, political, and social existence. His theory is extended by Kierkegaard, who explains the ironic role of anxiety in the process and who also shows that an array of other apparent contraries (e.g., the finite and the infinite, the temporal and the eternal, freedom and destiny) must also be held in the same kind of unity as that achieved by reason and the imagination if deliverance is to be achieved.

The Blake-Kierkegaard view of universal knowledge is formalized by Tillich. He conceptualizes man as a synthesis of reason and imagination possessing an ontological structure in which deliverance requires that tension be preserved between a set of egocentric and outer-world poles. Tillich's theory is easily applied to economic phenomena, as is illustrated by a discussion of man's reaction to sophisticated technology. It also provides a satisfactory definition of universal knowledge, which according to Foucault's strategy must now be co-ordinated with local knowledge.

Local knowledge is defined as the set of normative principles that should guide the Canadian conscience. It is an adaptation and an enrichment of universal knowledge in response to the specific characteristics of our own environment. We begin the task of identifying local knowledge by specifying, as a working hypothesis, that it has a primary theme.

In order to maintain the integrity of the nation, tension must be maintained between a set of fundamental bi-polar opposites that characterize Canadian existence.

Two comments about this hypothesis seem appropriate. First, if its plausibility can be demonstrated, the task of meshing universal and local knowledge is simplified because they share a common structure.

Second, it is advisable to provide some definitional precision in order to avoid ambiguity. Specifically, the word "integrity" carries the dual meaning of worthiness and wholeness, and "fundamental" implies that subset of all opposites in which a case can be made to support the sanctity of each pole. For example, efficiency and equality are fundamental opposites; good and evil are not. It is further hypothesized that the essence of Canadian local knowledge is captured in the work of Margaret Atwood, Harold Innis, and Alex Colville.

Atwood's major contribution is to identify three dimensions of opposition within the Canadian reality that should be given primacy: male-female, civilization-nature, and spatial-temporal. In her poetry and prose, she skilfully demonstrates that in the real world, these relationships are all characterized by domination, but that our integrity would be enhanced if it is replaced by a tension reflecting equality. She also suggests that there is a clustering of values, with maleness being associated with civilizational and spatial aspects of reality, whereas the female identifies with nature and temporal considerations. This clustering has useful methodological implications, for it signifies that the principles enunciated with respect to gender relationships have economic significance because they flow through to industrialization and the timing of resource development. Furthermore, it suggests that economic analysis should be approached with a new habit of mind in which dissonance between contraries is given prominence and nurtured rather than, as at present, suppressed.

Innis's work also supports the hypothesis. Early in his career as an economic historian, he developed a staples thesis which shows that Canada's development pattern has led to regional disparities and a heartland-hinterland dependency. Both are manifestations of a centre-margin opposition. Furthermore, government attempts to rectify the situation have been relatively unsuccessful and in fact have overlaid the economy with two additional burdens: chronic fiscal deficits that impinge upon the welfare of future generations and balance of payments deficits that lead to foreign ownership at the expense of Canadian independence. In his later work, he adds yet another dimension to his theory by demonstrating that spatially and temporally oriented communications systems are in fundamental opposition to each other. He observes that in all these dimensions, one element (i.e., the centre, the present generation, foreign interests, and spatially oriented communications systems) is dominant, most often because it is able to establish a monopoly position. His solution calls for the establishment of competing monopolies so that domination can be replaced by tension.

A third person who has articulated the nature of local knowledge is Alex Colville, a distinguished Canadian painter. To interpret his work it is necessary to understand that a serious work of art is a symbolic representation of a cogent idea, and it is this idea rather than the techniques of artistic design and production that interests us. Within this context it is observed that most of Colville's paintings have a common set of characteristics: two primary elements are held in non-dominating opposition; the idea springs from the tension of the relationship between the elements; the themes emphasize relationships between the sexes, technology and nature, and space-time interactions. Consequently his art tends to confirm the authenticity of both the hypothesis being examined and the dimensions identified by Atwood and Innis. Furthermore, it reinforces the notion that dissonance is the essence of reality and must be retained within the domain of any intellectual discipline which seeks to explain that reality.

From the foregoing, a preliminary conclusion emerges. Specifically, if Foucault's strategy has merit and if universal and local knowledges are as outlined, it follows that a normative Canadian economics discipline should be based on a dialectic methodology. In other words, since both subjugated knowledges have a dialectic structure, so also should any gestalt intellectual discipline that seeks to incorporate them.

Dialectic analysis is a common technique among historians and humanists but is foreign to most orthodox economists. However, a review of the procedure indicates that while it is complex, it is also capable of providing penetrating insights about Canadian economic processes and authenticating our hypothesized construct. For example, a line of reasoning is presented which suggests that confrontation between classes, a Marxian prognostication, has been prevented by the imposition of other dialectic relationships, all of which are characterized by domination: determinism over free will, the present over the future, the heartland over the hinterland. Within this framework, the objective of policy is again seen to be to eliminate the domination in these relationships, and the role of economic theory is to ascertain how this can best be accomplished.

In establishing this agenda, it is prudent to give priority to nationalist initiatives. To do so will necessitate an assessment of various instruments designed to generate a current account surplus. Furthermore, an industrial strategy needs to be formulated that will create a vigorous competitive environment and eliminate the distortions which currently exist in our economy: monopoly, excessive rent leakages, perverse transfer pricing, sectoral imbalances, premature resource exploitation, and the like. While this task is formidable in its own right, it is only a prelude to the evolution of a framework within which an array of oppressed elements of the Canadian reality can be nurtured.

The track record of nationalism has heretofore been rather dismal, in spite of the diligent efforts of many Canadians. However, there are aspects of the new paradigm that warrant cautious optimism about the future. It presents a perspective that is broadly based, indigenous, and egalitarian. Furthermore, its dialectic structure provides a means of overcoming what has been our major impediment: a lack of will. This reticence is attributed to our tendency to revere America, to prefer tolerance rather than assertiveness, to attach primary loyalties to regions, and to acquiese to the dictates of a derivative liberalism.

In the type of nationalism being advocated, all of these obstacles can be inverted to become lubricants. Perceived through the new paradigm, America is no longer a society to be emulated, tolerance is transformed into a militant demand to be tolerated, regionalism ceases to be a divisive force and becomes the basis for an enhanced resilience, and liberalism gives way to a new type of noble indigenous conservatism whose direction is guided by an interventionist government.

To participate constructively in this conversion, the economics discipline will need to abandon its aspiration to be a positive science and adopt a normative gestalt stance. There are precedents for radical changes such as this. For example, the discipline of physics has recently come to accept the counter-intuitive idea that the pursuit of truth is advanced by devising models of the universe in which time and space are treated as endogenous rather than exogenous variables (Hawking 1988). What is being proposed is an idea which is not nearly as profound but which is similarly counter-intuitive: in Canadian economics, the pursuit of optimality is advanced by devising models of society in which man is treated as an endogenous variable rather than as an axiom. Acceptance of this concept will transform the discipline. However, I believe that it is a transformation which must occur if the happiness of Canada's childhood is not to spoil the promise of its future.

References

Atwood, M. 1968. *The Animals in That Country*. Toronto: Oxford University Press.
– 1970. *The Journals of Susanna Moodie*. Toronto: Oxford University Press.
– 1972a. *Power Politics*. Toronto: Anansi.
– 1972b. *Surfacing*. Toronto: McClelland and Stewart.
– 1978. *Two-Headed Poems*. Toronto: Oxford University Press.
– 1984. *Interlunar*. Toronto: Oxford University Press.
Bagehot, W. 1888. *Economic Studies*. London: Longman Green.
Bentham, J. 1948. *An Introduction to the Principles of Morals and Legislation*. New York: Hafner.
Blake, W. *See* Ostriker 1977.
Blakely, B. 1983. The Pronunciation of Flesh: A Feminist Reading of Atwood's Poetry. In Grace and Weir.
Blaug, M. 1980. *The Methodology of Economics*. London: Cambridge University Press.
Breton, A. 1964. The economics of nationalism. *Journal of Political Economy* 72: 376–86.
Brinton, C.C. 1965. *Nietzsche*. New York: Harper & Row.
Burke, J.G., and M.C. Eakin, eds. 1979. *Technology and Change*. San Francisco: Boyd and Fraser.
Burnett, D. 1983. *Colville*. Toronto: McClelland and Stewart.
Cain, S. 1984. Keynes on Change, Reason and Expectations. Unpublished master's thesis, University of Calgary.
Caldwell, B.J. 1982. *Beyond Positivism: Economic Methodology in the Twentieth Century*. London: George Allen and Unwin.

– ed. 1984. *Appraisal and Criticism in Economics*. Boston: Allen and Unwin.

Canadian Broadcasting Corporation (CBC). 1987. *William Blake: Prophet of the New Age*. Toronto: Ideas Transcript, 4107–97.

Carey, J.W. 1981. Culture, Geography and Communications. In Melody et al.

Cox, H. 1966. *The Secular City*. New York: Macmillan.

– 1969. *The Feast of Fools*. Cambridge: Harvard University Press.

Crean, S., and M. Rioux. 1982. *Two Nations*. Toronto: Lorimer.

Creighton, D. 1981. Harold Adams Innis – An Appraisal. In Melody et al.

Daly, H.E. 1980. *Economics, Ecology, Ethics*. San Francisco: Freeman.

Davey, F. 1984. *Margaret Atwood: A Feminist Poetics*. Vancouver: Talonbooks.

Davidson, A.E., and C.N. Davidson, eds. 1981. *Margaret Atwood: Essays in Criticism*. Toronto: Anansi.

Davidson, P. 1977. Post-Keynesian Monetary Theory and Inflation. In Weintraub.

Deane, P. 1978. *The Evolution of Economic Ideas*. Cambridge: Cambridge University Press.

Deleuze, G., and F. Guattari. 1983. *Anti-Oedipus: Capitalism and Schizophrenia*. Minneapolis: University of Minnesota Press.

Diesing, P. 1971. *Patterns of Discovery in the Social Sciences*. New York: Aldine.

Donington, R. 1963. *Wagner's Ring and its Symbols*. London: Faber.

Eliot, T.S. 1964. *Collected Poems: 1909–1962*. New York: Harcourt Brace.

Ellul, J. 1964. *The Technological Society*. New York: Knopf.

– 1979. The Technological Order. In Burke and Eakin.

Foucault, M. 1979. *Discipline and Punish*. New York: Random House.

Frank, A.G. 1967. *Capitalism and Underdevelopment in Latin America*. New York: Monthly Review Press.

Frye, N. 1947. *Fearful Symmetry*. London: Oxford University Press.

– 1971. *The Bush Garden*. Toronto: Anansi.

– 1981. *The Great Code*. Toronto: Academic Press.

– 1990. *Words with Power*. Markham: Penguin.

Fukuyama, F. 1989. The End of History. *Globe and Mail*, 1–15 December.

Galbraith, J.K. 1967. *The New Industrial State*. New York: Signet.

Georgescu-Roegen, N. 1971. *The Entropy Law and the Economic Process*. Cambridge: Harvard University Press.

Gordon, C., ed. 1980. *Power/Knowledge*. Brighton: Harvester Press.

Gouldner, A.W. 1976. *The Dialectic of Ideology and Technology*. New York: Seabury Press.

– 1980. *The Two Marxisms*. New York: Seabury Press.

Government of Canada. 1986. *Royal Commission on the Economic Union and Development Prospects for Canada*. Ottawa: Supply and Services.

Grace, S. 1980. *Violent Duality*. Montreal: Véhicule Press.

Grace, S., and L. Weir, eds. 1983. *Margaret Atwood: Language, Text and System*. Vancouver: University of British Columbia Press.

Grant, G. 1965. *Lament for a Nation*. Ottawa: Carleton University Press.

– 1969. *Technology and Empire*. Toronto: Anansi.

– 1986. *Technology and Justice*. Toronto: Anansi.

Guédon, M. 1983. Surfacing: Amerindian Themes and Shamanism. In Grace and Weir.

Hawking, S.W. 1988. *A Brief History of Time*. Toronto: Bantam.

Hayek, F. 1973. *Economic Freedom and Representative Government*. London: Institute of Economic Affairs.

Heilbroner, R.L. 1980. *Marxism: For and Against*. New York: Norton.

Heiss, R. 1975. *Hegel, Kierkegaard, Marx*. New York: Dell.

Hollander, S. 1977. Adam Smith and the Self-Interest Axiom. *The Journal of Law and Economics* 20: 133–52.

Hood, W.A. 1972. The Aristotlean Versus the Heideggerian Approach to the Problem of Technology. In Mitcham and Mackey.

Hook, S. 1976. *From Hegel to Marx*. New York: Humanities Press.

Innis, H.A. 1936. *Settlement and the Mining Frontier*. Toronto: Macmillan.

– 1940. *The Cod Fisheries*. New Haven: Yale University Press.

– 1950. *Empire and Communications*. London: Oxford University Press.

– 1956. *The Fur Trade in Canada*. Toronto: University of Toronto Press.

– 1964. *The Bias of Communication*. Toronto: University of Toronto Press.

– 1971. *A History of the Canadian Pacific Railway*. Toronto: University of Toronto Press.

Israel, J. 1979. *The Language of Dialectics and the Dialectics of Language*. Copenhagen: Munksgaard.

Jacobs, J. 1984. *Cities and the Wealth of Nations*. New York: Random House.

Jay, M. 1973. *The Dialectic Imagination*. Boston: Little, Brown.

– 1984. *Marxism and Totality*. Berkeley: University of California Press.

John Paul II. 1981. *Laborem Exercens*. Ottawa: Canadian Council of Catholic Bishops.

Kant, I. 1905. *Critique of Pure Reason*. New York: Collier.

Katouzian, H. 1980. *Ideology and Method in Economics*. London: Macmillan.

Kazantzakis, N. 1957. *The Last Temptation of Christ*. New York: Simon and Schuster.

Keynes, J.M. 1920. *The Economic Consequences of the Peace*. New York: Harcourt Brace.

– 1935. *The General Theory of Employment, Interest, and Money*. New York: Harcourt Brace.

– 1951. *Essays in Biography*. London: Macmillan.

Kierkegaard, S. 1946. *Concluding Unscientific Postscript to the Philosophical Fragments*. In *A Kierkegaard Anthology*, ed. R. Bretall. Princeton: Princeton University Press.

– 1957. *The Concept of Dread*. Princeton: Princeton University Press.

– 1959. *Either/Or*. Garden City: Doubleday.

– 1967. *Journals and Papers*. Bloomington: Indiana University Press.

Kroker, A. 1985. *Technology and the Canadian Mind*. Montreal: New World.

Laing, R.D. 1959. *The Divided Self*. New York: Pantheon.

Lane, F.C., ed. 1953. *Enterprise and Secular Change*. Homewood: Irwin.

Langer, S. 1953. *Feeling and Form*. New York: Scribner.

Lee, D. 1974. Cadence, Country Silence. *boundary 2*, 3, no. 1: 151–68.

– 1977. *Savage Fields*. Toronto: Anansi.

Leontief, W. 1982. Academic Economics. *Science 217*.

Locke, J. 1924. *An Essay Concerning Human Understanding*. Oxford: Clarendon Press.

– 1967. *Two Treatises on Civil Government*. Cambridge: Cambridge University Press.

Macfarlane, A. 1979. *The Origins of English Individualism*. New York: Cambridge University Press.

Machlup, F. 1978. *Methodology of Economics and Other Social Sciences*. New York: Academic Press.

MacLennan, H. 1945. *Two Solitudes*. Toronto: Collins.

Macpherson, C.B. 1962. *The Political Theory of Possessive Individualism*. Oxford: Clarendon Press.

– 1985. *The Rise and Fall of Economic Justice*. Oxford: Oxford University Press.

Malahat Review. 1977. 41.

Mann, T. 1986. *Doctor Faustus*. Markham: Penguin.

Mansell, R.L., and M.B. Percy. 1989. *Strength through Adversity*. Montreal: C.D. Howe.

Marcuse, H. 1964. *One-Dimensional Man*. Boston: Beacon Press.

Martin, B. 1971. *The Existential Theory of Paul Tillich*. New Haven: College Press.

Marx, K. 1913. *A Contribution to the Critique of Political Economy*. Chicago: Charles H. Kerr.

– 1964. *Economic and Philosophic Manuscripts of 1844*. New York: International.

Marx, K., and F. Engels. 1970. *The German Ideology*. New York: International.

McCloskey, D.N. 1983. The Rhetoric of Economics. *Journal of Economic Literature* 21: 481–517.

McCombs, J. 1988. *Critical Essays on Margaret Atwood*. Boston: Hall.

McLuhan, M. 1969. *Counter Blast*. Toronto: McClelland and Stewart.

Melody, W.H., L. Salter, and P. Heyer, eds. 1981. *Culture, Communications and Dependency*. Norwood: Ablex Publishing.

Mitcham, C., and R. Mackey, eds. 1972. *Philosophy and Technology*. New York: Free Press.

Mill, J.S. 1968. *Essays on Some Unsettled Questions of Political Economy*. New York: Augustus M. Kelly.

Mini, P.V. 1974. *Philosophy and Economics*. Gainesville: The University Presses of Florida.

Mirowski, P. 1988. *Against Mechanism*. New Jersey: Rowman & Littlefield.

Musgrave, A. 1984. Unreal Assumptions in Economic Theory: The F-Twist Untwisted. In Caldwell.

Naylor, R.T. 1975. *The History of Canadian Business*. Toronto: Lorimer.

Neill, R. 1972. *A New Theory of Value*. Toronto: University of Toronto Press.

Newton, I. 1968. *The Mathematical Principles of Natural Philosophy*. London: Dawsons.

Orwell, G. 1966. *Keep the Aspidistra Flying*. Harmondsworth: Penguin.

Ostriker, A., ed. 1977. *William Blake: The Complete Poems*. Markham: Penguin.

Parry, G. 1978. *John Locke*. London: Allen and Unwin.

Polanyi, K. 1944. *The Great Transformation*. Boston: Beacon Press.

Porter, M.E. 1991. *Canada at the Crossroads*. Ottawa: Business Council on National Issues and the Government of Canada.

Porter, R.C. 1982. The New Approach to Wilderness Preservation through Benefit-Cost Analysis. *Journal of Environmental Economics and Management* no. 1: 59–80.

Punter, D. 1982. *Blake, Hegel and Dialectic*. Amsterdam: Rodopi.

Pynchon, T. 1973. *Gravity's Rainbow*. New York: Viking.

Reder, M. 1982. Chicago Economics: Permanence and Change. *Journal of Economic Literature* 20: 1–38.

Reinitz, R. 1980. *Irony and Consciousness*. Toronto: Associated University Presses.

Rifkin, J. 1980. *Entropy*. New York: Viking.

Robbins, L. 1935. *Essay on the Nature and Significance of Economic Science*. London: Macmillan.

Rogin, L. 1956. *The Meaning and Validity of Economic Theory*. New York: Harper.

Rosenberg, J.H. 1984. *Margaret Atwood*. Boston: Twayne.

Roszak, T. 1979. *Person/Planet*. New York: Doubleday.

– 1986. *The Cult of Information*. New York: Pantheon.

Rotstein, A. 1973. *The Precarious Homestead*. Toronto: New Press.

– 1978. "Is There an English-Canadian Nationalism?" Toronto: Walter Gordon Lecture Series.

Schumacher, E.F. 1973. *Small is Beautiful*. New York: Harper & Row.

Scitovsky, T. 1976. *The Joyless Economy*. Oxford: Oxford University Press.

Second Vatican Ecumenical Council. 1966. *Pastoral Constitution on the Church in the Modern World*.

Senior, N.W. 1951. *An Outline of the Science of Political Economy*. New York: Kelley.

Sheridan, A. 1980. *Michel Foucault*. London: Tavistock.

Simeon, R. 1988. Meech Lake and Shifting Conceptions of Canadian Federalism. *Canadian Public Policy*, supplement.

Skinner, B.F. 1966. *Science and Human Behavior*. New York: Free Press.

– 1971. *Beyond Freedom and Dignity*. New York: Bantam.

Smart, B. 1983. *Foucault, Marxism and Criticism*. London: Routledge & Kegan Paul.

Smith, A. 1937. *An Inquiry into the Nature and Causes of the Wealth of Nations*. New York: Random House.

– 1963. The History of Astronomy. In *The Works of Adam Smith*, vol. V. Aalen: Oho Zeller.

– 1976. *The Theory of Moral Sentiments*. Oxford: Clarendon.

Spiethoff, A. 1953. Pure Theory and Economic Gestalt Theory. In Lane.

Strauss, L. 1959. *What Is Political Philosophy?* Glencoe: Free Press.

Thompson, H.F. 1965. Adam Smith's Philosophy of Science. *Quarterly Journal of Economics* 79: 212–33.

Tillich, P. 1951. *Systematic Theology I*. Chicago: University of Chicago Press.

Toffler, A. 1990. *Powershift*. New York: Bantam.

Veblen, T. 1934. *The Theory of the Leisure Class*. New York: Random House.

Viner, J. 1960. The Intellectual History of Laissez Faire. *Journal of Law and Economics* 3: 45–69.

Watkins, M. 1978. The Economics of Nationalism and the Nationality of Economics. *The Canadian Journal of Economics* 11, no. 4, supplement.

Weber, M. 1985. *The Protestant Ethic and the Spirit of Capitalism*. London: Unwin.

Weintraub, S., ed. 1977. *Modern Economic Thought*. Oxford: Basil Blackwell.

Westfall, W. 1989. Review of *The Century that Made Us*, by G. Woodcock. In *Globe and Mail*, 9 September.

White, H.V. 1973. *Metahistory*. Baltimore: John Hopkins University Press.

Wicksteed, P.H. 1933. *The Common Sense of Political Economy*. London: Routledge & Kegan Paul.

Woodcock, G. 1989. *The Century that Made Us*. Don Mills: Oxford University Press.

Index

analytic domain: and pure theory, 4–5; and Smith and Ricardo, 14

anxiety of existential disruption, 54, 66

art theory: works of art, symbols, semblance, and virtual space, 74–6

Atwood, M., 59–67, 123; and Colville, 83; on dissonance, 66; and feminism, 61–2; and the *idea of progress*, 62–5; and Innis, 72; and inversion, 92; and the *Journals of Susanna Moodie*, 60–1; and Kierkegaard, 66; and nationalism, 63–4, 66; poetic themes, 60; on stoicism, escapism, and transcendence, 64–5; and technology, 62–3

Blake, W., 44–9, 121–2; and the *idea of progress*, 46, 48; on the industrial revolution and transcendence, 45; on tense dialectic relationships, 49; on work, 47–8

classical economics, 11–17, 120

Colville, A., 74–84, 124; and Atwood and Innis, 83; characteristics of paintings, 76; and dissonance, 83; interpretations of paintings, 77–82; and thought concreteness, 87

constructive rationalism, 11

cultural penetration: high, mass, and popular cultures, 109; and inversions, 109

Descartes, R., 7–9; and Blake, 45. *See also* Ricardo, D.

deterministic forces, 23, 120; erosion theories, 29–32; global theories, 24–7; technological theories, 27–9

dialectic analysis: Aristotle and Heidegger on intrinsic technology, 89; and Canadian economic development, 124; components of (totality, intrinsic relations, process, and relatedness), 86–95; and the *idea of progress*, 85, 87–8; and individuation, 94; and inversion, 91–2, 109–12, 119; objectives of, 85–6

economic policies: and the current account dilemma, 114–5; exchange rates, protection, and competition policy as mechanisms to achieve balance, 115–7
education systems: and the dialectic between reason and imagination, 102; and technology, 30–1
Ellul, J.: on determinism, 27–8; on technical reason, 56
end of history debate, 100

Foucault, M., 33, 121; on discipline, 38; on the insurrection of sub-jugated knowledges, 41, 121; on knowledge and truth, 41; and Nietzsche, 34–6
Frankfurt School, 100

generic axioms, 5–6
gestalt theory, 4, 21, 49, 72, 125
Grant, G., 31, 108; and Innis, 70

idea of progress: and Atwood, 62–3, 65; and Blake, 46, 48; and Canadian subservience, 109; challenges to, viii; and classical economics, 11; and the dialectic method, 85, 87–8, 95; and discrimination, 118; and erosion theories, 29–30; evolution of, 6–11; and Innis, 71, 73; and Keynes, 20; and nationalism, 107, 112; origins, vii; and phenomenal forces, 23; and Smith, 12–14; and Tillich, 53, 57
imagination, 103. *See also* art theory; Blake, W.
Innis, H., 67–74, 123; and Atwood, 72; and Colville, 83; on communi-cations theory, 71; on empire, bias, and competition, 73; on govern-ment policies and staples development, 69–70; and Grant, 70; and the *idea of progress*, 71, 73; on monopoly, 71; on orthodox economics and gestalt theory, 72; and the staples thesis, 68; and tense dialectics, 67, 70, 73; and thought concreteness, 87
insurrection of subjugated knowledges, 41, 101, 121
inversion, 91–2, 109–12, 119

justice, 53, 54–6, 118

Keynes, J.M., 20–2, 120; and the *idea of progress*, 20
Kierkegaard, S., 49–52, 122; and Atwood, 66; on dread, 51; and tense dialectics, 51; on truth, 51

Marx, K.: on class consciousness, 97; on determinism, 25–6; on dia-lectic materialism, 96; on individuation, 94–5; on revolutionary pre-requisites, 98; on technology, 100
myth of deliverance, 44

nationalism: barriers, 108–12, 118; elements of a dialectic theory, 102; feasibility, 113–9
– as a prerequisite for: the enhancement of the education system, 102–3; the enrichment of French-English relationships, 106; the realign-ment of spatial and temporal priorities, 104; the reassessment of centre and margin issues, 104–6

– summary, 124–5
neo-classical economics, 17–20
Newton, I., 9–10; and Blake, 45
Nietzsche, F., 34–6

ontology. *See* Tillich, P.
orthodox economics: contributions of Descartes, 7–9, Keynes, 20–2, Newton, 9–10, Ricardo, 14–16, Smith, 11–14; definition of, 3; domain of, 4; generic axioms, 5–6; as ideology, 40–1; Innis's criticism of, 72; limitations of, 5; and power relationships, 40; summary, 120

phenomena: and noumena, 23; as output of economic processes, 33. *See also* deterministic forces
positive economics, 18–19; and Smith, 14

religion, 7, 11, 43–5; festivals and fantasies, 30; and scientific understanding, 45. *See also* Blake, W.; Kierkegaard, S.; Tillich, P.
Ricardo, D., x, 11, 14–16

Skinner, B.F., 26–7
Smith, A., x, 11–14, 100, 120; and the *idea of progress*, 12–14
staples thesis, 68–9, 123

tense dialectics, 49, 51, 54, 59, 67, 73
Tillich, P., 52–7, 122; on the anxiety of existential disruption, 54, 66; and the *idea of progress*, 53, 57; on ontology, 53–4; and preference-shaping technologies, 55–7; on reason and imagination, 52; on self-elevation and economic man, 55

wisdom: as a synthesis of rationalism and spiritualism, 30